The Intelligible Universe

This book is an investigation of cosmological or causal arguments for the existence of God, and a setting-out and defence of one such argument. After an unsympathetic treatment of the wide-spread view that arguments for the existence of God are pointless, since religious belief needs no rational justification on grounds independent of itself, the usual objections to cosmological arguments for theism are set out in detail.

It is a principal contention of the book that cosmological arguments are most fruitfully considered against a background of discussion of the theory of knowledge. Two accounts of the nature of knowledge in particular are stressed and contrasted. The first has been defended especially by empiricist philosophers; it is argued not only that it leads to very paradoxical conclusions for history, science, and the knowledge of other minds, but that it is actually self-destructive. The second, it is argued, has perfectly satisfactory and unproblematic consequences for these kinds of inquiry, but leads inevitably to a definite conception of the nature and structure of the world.

Hugo A. Meynell shows that the best way of accounting for the existence of a world of such a nature and structure is the *fiat* of an intelligent will; in fact, of something like what has always been called 'God'. This thesis is defended against the objections to cosmological arguments summarised earlier in the book; and a moral is drawn about the positive relation of theistic belief to the scientific outlook.

Hugo A. Meynell is Senior Lecturer in the Departments of Philosophy and of Theology and Religious Studies at the University of Leeds. His previous books are *Sense, Nonsense and Christianity, Grace versus Nature, The New Theology and Modern Theologians, God and the World, An Introduction to the Philosophy of Bernard Lonergan* and *Freud, Marx and Morals*. He has published several articles in journals on philosophical and theological subjects.

THE INTELLIGIBLE UNIVERSE

A Cosmological Argument

HUGO A. MEYNELL

BARNES & NOBLE BOOKS
TOTOWA, NEW JERSEY

First published in the U.S.A. 1982 by
BARNES & NOBLE BOOKS
81, Adams Drive, Totowa,
New Jersey, 07512
ISBN 0–389–20253–3

Printed in Hong Kong

The things that were to be, and those that have been and now are
no more and all things that are now, and the things that are to
be — all these Mind has set in order. (Anaxagoras)

I understand objective to mean what is independent of our sensation, intuition and imagination, and of all construction of mental
pictures out of memories of earlier sensations, but not what is independent of the reason, — for what are things independent of
the reason? To answer that would be as much as to judge without
judging, or to wash the fur without wetting it. (Frege)

Contents

Introduction

Arguments for the existence of God may be divided into two kinds, those which argue from a definition of God directly to his existence, without taking into account the world of our experience; and those which argue from some very general feature of the world of our experience to the existence of something supposed to account for this, which is then assumed or argued to be identical with God. It is arguments of the latter sort which are generally termed 'cosmological', as opposed to those of the first, which are called 'ontological'. Among arguments which are 'cosmological' in this sense, those which argue from the presence of order or design in the world to the existence of an orderer or designer of the world are usually treated separately, as 'physico-theological' arguments. The terminology is due to Kant;[1] and has been, along with the division between types of argument which it marks, commonly retained by subsequent philosophers. The threefold division seems satisfactory on the face of it, and I shall follow it. I shall be dealing with cosmological arguments in the restricted sense, and shall only refer to ontological and physico-theological arguments incidentally, as throwing light on cosmological arguments.

The plan which will be followed by the book is as follows. After a brief and not very respectful notice of the contention that it is pointless to try to construct arguments for God's existence, standard forms of cosmological argument will be set out together with the usual objections to them. It appears to me that the point of cosmological arguments cannot be adequately grasped without raising the question of the nature of human knowledge in general; this will be done in the following section. Finally, a version of cosmological argument will be presented against this background; this will be related to traditional forms of the argument, and objections to it reviewed.

1 On the Alleged Unimportance of Arguments for God's Existence

It is often maintained that arguments for the existence of God are not really of any significance for religious faith. If a person is untouched by religious feeling or the disposition to worship, or is not responsive to the claims of any religious revelation, it is said, argument will certainly not make him so. If he is, on the contrary, disposed to engage in the practices and related discourse constitutive of a religion, and thus to have a real relationship to the God (if any) of that religion, such arguments will be superfluous. One either plays some religious language-game, participates in some religious form of life, or one does not. Philosophical argument can have, or at least ought to have, no bearing on the matter either way; except to show that philosophical argument has no such bearing.[1] Even if such arguments as purport to prove, or to render probable, the existence of some 'transcendent Being', or what have you, did succeed, they would only provide the metaphysician with an abstraction who had nothing to do with the God of the worshipper.

Three versions of this position seem worth mentioning: those that take their stand respectively on revelation, religious experience, and existential commitment. The first is to the effect that God's revelation of himself alone justifies man's speech about him, and makes justification from the human side at best unnecessary, at worst blasphemous. Since God has in fact provided a revelation of his existence and nature, only two responses are available for man; either he accepts the revelation in faith, or he rejects it in sin. To expect human reason to be able to establish whether there exists a God who might have revealed himself is to

1

take no account of the darkened and depraved nature of that reason as proclaimed in that very revelation. Furthermore, for one who already accepts God's revelation, arguments on supposedly neutral grounds for his existence can only be a piece of play-acting; for one who sinfully neglects the revelation, they cannot possibly carry any conviction. And even if some 'proof' of the existence of a 'God' were accepted as valid, the 'God' thus 'proved' would merely be a figment of proud and assertive human reason, and consequently have nothing to do with the true God, who is essentially and ineluctably he who demands faith, and is to be apprehended exclusively in and through faith.[2]

The trouble with this position is just that it is impossible to see why, if such a privilege is claimed for one alleged revelation, it should not be claimed for any other. In fact, of course, it is notorious that there are a number of competing claims as to what the sources of divine revelation are, and what authorities, if any, have the capacity to provide the correct interpretation of what may be inferred from those sources in disputed cases. If the rival sources and authorities agreed, or disagreed only insignificantly, on what ought to be believed about God or other important matters, the problem would perhaps not be so serious; but the disagreements are obvious and acute. How, on the account given, is one even in principle to go about determining which of the conflicting claimants, if any, to be the unique source or the unique interpreter of the source of divine revelation, is to be believed?

It may alternatively be argued that direct apprehension of God is to be had in religious experience, and that it is this fact which renders otiose arguments of the traditional kind to establish his existence.[3] If sense-experience is allowed to furnish us with evidence of a world which exists apart from our sense-experience, and would exist even if we had no such sense-experience, why should not religious experience, it may be asked, similarly provide us with adequate grounds for belief in God? This suggestion is liable to the following objections. One may understand the proposition 'I have an experience of X' in two senses, in one of which it is implied that X is something real, which would have existed even if I had not had the experience; and in the other of which it is not so implied. That people have experience of God in the second sense may be acknowledged for the purposes of the present discussion. But that they have experience of God in the second sense does not imply that they have experience of him in the first; it has to be asked why God should not be analogous rather to the pink rats 'seen' by the patient suffering from *delirium tremens*, than to the white rats seen in the course of duty by the sober and diligent worker in the psychology laboratory. What reasons do we have for believing that our sensations are at least charac- teristically of material objects really existing in the world? Do the same apply to our experiences of God? There are at least some *prima facie* reasons for supposing that they do not. To believe in real material objects is to acknowledge that our present and past experience and practice must, if we are to prosper, be a guide to our future experience and practice. But belief in material objects in this sense could hardly be given up with impunity; whereas belief in God quite palpably can be and often is so – unless perhaps one appeals to some future life, which may well be felt to involve more problems than belief in God itself.[4]

Theologians influenced by existentialism are apt to argue that belief in God depends ultimately on an act of preference, for which there is no compelling justification. They may plead that, if one concludes that it is a matter of choice, it is important to be clear about the kind of choice which is involved.[5] An element of voluntariness enters into the formation and maintenance of every belief to which one is not compelled by strict logic, and usually one has to decide how much weight to give to conflicting con- siderations. In the case of most men for most of history, beliefs about metaphysical and religious matters have been determined entirely by their social environment, and there has been little or no scope for personal decision. But where there is a fundamental clash between such beliefs within a culture, people have to make up their own minds, and to 'find that commitment which prom- ises to realise their best potentialities, and in that sense to become their true selves'.[6] Theists will usually insist that to find one's deepest self is to find God, while atheists retort that it is to see through the religious illusion; philosophical argument cannot settle the issue in either direction. It can properly clarify the nature of existential choice, and show why one cannot avoid mak- ing it; but it cannot determine what that choice is to be.

The difficulty here is much the same as that about religious ex- perience; the logical outcome of this view seems to be that 'God', as not fulfilling the usual conditions of shared existence in an inter-personal and public world, becomes nothing more than an internal accusative of verbs signifying existential commitment. Short of positive grounds for such belief, it may be concluded, one ought not to believe in a 'God' supposed to exist outside the mind of existentially committed human subjects, to 'exist' at all in fact in any non-Pickwickian sense. 'It is by reference to this inescapable demand for grounds that the presumption of atheism is justified. If it is to be established that there is a God, then we have to have good grounds for believing that this is indeed so.'[7] 'The impossibility of any rational argument for belief, supposing it really obtained, would be a strong and quite rational argument against belief.'[8] Belief that arguments for the existence of God do not work has led many theists to the conviction that they do not matter; sceptics may be forgiven for maintaining that it ought to have led rather to the conviction that theism is false.

It is often pointed out that argument is not the only or the main factor which makes people religious or irreligious, to believe that God exists or that he does not. But it by no means follows that argument has and ought to have nothing at all to do with the matter. Even if arguments for the existence of God do not generally produce conversion, they may yet have the function of convincing those already converted, or perhaps otherwise disposed to conversion, that they are not crazy.[9] To be transported by 'experience of God', or by the thrill of existential commitment, is one thing; to be in a position to make the reasonable judgement that there is a God is quite another, and, in the case of this emotional state as in other similar ones, the thoughtful person will be chary of the conclusions to which he is borne under its influence, until these have been rationally justified.[10]

And if supporting arguments do and ought to sustain conviction, in religion as in other matters, the absence of such argument quite properly tends to weaken or dissolve it. The point has been well put by Austin Farrer:

It is commonly said that if rational argument is so seldom the cause of conviction, philosophical apologists must be wasting their shot. The premise is true, but the conclusion does not follow. For though argument does not create conviction, lack of it destroys belief. What seems to be proved may not be embraced; but what no one shows the ability to defend is quickly abandoned. Rational argument does not create belief, but it maintains a climate in which belief may flourish.[11]

There is some sociological evidence to support this view. On the basis of a survey conducted in Nottingham of people's reports of their religious experiences, it was concluded that many more people than is usually supposed have such experiences, but are apt to dismiss them as illusory or due to nervous disorder on the assumption that the whole trend of modern knowledge tells against their validity. 'It may well be in our society this whole vast area of religious or transcendental experience may be largely hidden away, because so many people lack sufficiently credible "available systems of significance" to which can be attached their deeply felt inner perceptions.' [12] If on the contrary they were to be convinced, by the traditional theistic arguments or something like them, that there is good reason to believe that there is a real being, which exists independently of human religious feelings, but which justifies and rightly evokes those feelings, this surely would quite properly encourage them to allow such feelings to develop, and to permeate their views of the world and of life as a whole, rather than to suppress or inhibit them.

John Macquarrie has argued that a new style of natural theology is needed, based on Heidegger's existentialism; he maintains that if, in the manner of the older natural theology, God is supposed to be shown to exist as the conclusion of an inference, or as the postulate of a successful explanatory hypothesis, he is *eo ipso* debased to a mere object within the world, and his transcendence is compromised. [13] It seems to me that an important task of philosophical theology, and one which is often neglected, is showing what relevance belief in God, for better or for worse, has to human living in all its aspects; in implementing this task, one could very well take Heidegger's work, with its impressive analysis of human consciousness as more or less authentic, as one's starting-point. But this by no means implies that the question whether there is good reason to believe that there is a God, or that there is not, ought to be abandoned. And as J. J. Shepherd remarks, if the older type of natural theology did make God a part of the cosmos it would be inadequate from both the philosophical and the religious point of view; yet 'given that God is not nothing it cannot avoid making him part of the totality of what is'. [14]

I conclude that those believers in God who think that arguments for the existence of God are irrelevant to their position are seriously mistaken, unless indeed the 'God' in 'whom' they 'believe' is totally different from what has been traditionally designated by the term. Those who hold that it is possible or desirable thus to 'rescue God from metaphysical captivity'[15] should ponder whether the effect of such efforts is not rather either to trivialise talk about God, or deprive it of all justification. The widely advertised alleged failure of all traditional forms of argument for God's existence is thus not to be regarded with complacency by theists. If there is no argument, which does not more or less blatantly or covertly assume what it sets out to prove, which makes it more reasonable to suppose, on the basis of premisses and forms of reasoning acceptable in principle to all reasonable people, that there is a God than that there is not, then one ought to be an atheist; or one ought to regard theistic religion as an entirely autonomous and self-justifying activity, without metaphysical implications or commitments — which may well be felt after all to amount to much the same thing.

2 Standard Arguments and Counter-Arguments

The simplest form of cosmological or causal argument for God's existence may be set out as follows: 'In the world every thing, event, or state of affairs has a cause, its cause in turn has another cause, and so on and so on. The series of causes cannot be infinite. So there must be a first or uncaused cause of all the things, events and states of affairs that constitute the world; and this is what we call God.'

Objection 1. That the causal series must have a first term is an unjustified assumption. Why should it not be infinite? Why should we not say that the things of which we are directly aware are caused by other things, and so on indefinitely?[1] If it were argued that since no series can be infinite, the causal series cannot be so, the premiss of that argument would be demonstrably false. The mathematical series within which occur the numbers ... 1/100, 1/10, 1, 10, 100 ... has no first or last term. Why should not the same apply to the series of causes?[2] I exist because of my parents, they exist because of theirs, and so on back to the emergence of the most primitive forms of life in the Pre-Cambrian age, and beyond. Why should there have been any first term in this causal series?

And the example taken draws attention to another objection. Most of my ancestors no longer exist. Even if there were a first term in the series of causes, what adequate reason could there be for asserting that it exists now? We know by experience that effects may exist long after their causes have perished.[3] A first cause which once existed, but no longer does so, would not be God in anything approaching the usual sense of the term.

It may be protested that what are at issue are the conditions for the existence of anything which have to obtain simultaneously with it, and could not be destroyed without the thing itself being so. For example, my existence here and now is dependent on that of certain organic compounds, their existence on that of certain chemical elements, and so on. But why should this kind of causal series stand any more in need of a first term than the one already discussed?

It may be said, as it was by Thomas Aquinas,[4] that if there were not a first cause, no effect would exist; to take away the first cause would be to take away all the other causes in the series which are its effects. But if there *is* no first cause, nothing is removed in removing the first cause.[5] Those who advance this argument seem to confuse an infinite series with one which is very long but finite. It may be granted that, however long a series of causes in which there is a first term, given that the first term did not exist or obtain, the ultimate effect would not exist or obtain either. But whether there need be a first term at all is precisely what is in question.[6]

Objection 2. Even granted the premiss that every event has a cause, it cannot validly be inferred that there is just one cause which is the cause of every event. If there were a sound argument which established that there was *at least one* first cause, it would still have to be shown that there is *only* one, as a theist must maintain.[7] As a matter of fact, we have reason *not* to believe that the various causal series with which we are acquainted tend to converge as we follow them from their effects to their causes. For example, a man has two parents, four grandparents, and eight great-grandparents; and there are a number of simultaneous factual conditions on which his existence depends at each moment, every one of which depends on so many more, and so on. At that rate, even if it were admitted that *every* causal series had a first term, this would be quite consistent with there being a *plurality* of first causes of the various causal series constitutive of the world.[8]

It is easy to miss the gap in the argument here because of a fallacy well known to logicians, called by them the 'quantifier shift', which is apt to be obscured by ordinary language. It is one thing to state the truism that every wife has a husband; quite another to make the astonishing, and patently false, claim, that there is one particular man who is husband to all wives. From the statement 'Every girl loves some sailor', it should not be inferred that there is some one sailor, let us say Lord Nelson, who is loved by all girls. In such cases, the ambiguity latent in such phrases as

'*a* husband', '*some* sailor', deceives no one; but it is a very different matter when common sense and everyday experience provide
no immediate check on the results of reasoning.

*Objection 3. To argue to God as cause of the world is to neglect the possibil-
ity that causal relations are rather imposed by the human understanding
upon the events of the world, than characteristic of events prior to and independently of human understanding of them.* It does seem that our disposition to look for causal explanations of events is very much
dictated by our interests and concerns. What we are inclined
loosely to call 'the' cause of some event tends to be that which, if
we had prevented it, we would also have prevented the event; or
that which, if we can bring about, we can bring about the event.
This is the kind of way in which we speak of 'the' cause or causes
of smallpox or nettlerash, or of someone's success as a teacher or a
businessman. Furthermore, as was made clear particularly by the
work of David Hume,[9] the casual relation between events is not
strictly speaking something which can be perceived. I may perceive the brick making its impact on the window at one moment,
and the window smashed at the next; but I cannot, however sedu-
lously I scrutinise the sequence of events, actually perceive the
one event causing the other. Is not the most probable conclusion
to be drawn from these facts that causality is rather imposed by
the human mind on the flux of phenomena than a state of affairs
which is in things apart from human inquiry? Should we not
agree with the dictum that 'belief in the causal nexus' as such a
real state of affairs 'is superstition'?[10] And at this rate, as Kant
above all argued, to try to argue for a real first cause of things in
general, or of the empirical world as a whole, is to misuse a
faculty whose proper and everyday employment is to impose intelligibility on patterns of events *within* that world.

*Objection 4. It has to be shown why the existence of the universe itself, or of
some part or aspect of it, cannot be a mere 'brute fact' without explanation or
cause. If it be objected that this cannot be the case with the universe or any
aspect of it, it has to be shown why the same does not apply to God.* If it is
insisted that the world or some aspect of it needs to be explained
by reference to some principle external to the world, it may reasonably be asked how *that* is to be explained; and infinite regress
seems inevitable. But if it is retorted that that which is invoked to

explain the world or some aspect of it does not itself need explanation, then how this can be so has to be shown. It will not do to
treat the principle of universal causality, given that one is in a position to invoke it at all, like 'a hired cab which we dismiss when
we have reached our destination', as Schopenhauer expressed
it.[11] 'If it is puzzling that *anything* exists, it should seem puzzling
that God does; if a certain feature's presence in the universe is
puzzling, then it should seem puzzling that it, or that which gives
rise to it, should be present in God. In neither case is the explanation complete.'[12] One may well conclude, with Hume's Philo,
that to look outside the cosmic system for an explanation of it, or
of any aspect of it, is to excite an insatiable appetite.[13]

In response to this difficulty, it is often maintained that God's
nature differs from that of the world and all its constituents in that
his existence is 'necessary', while theirs is merely 'contingent'. If
God necessarily exists, his existence will not demand explanation
in the same sort of way as does the existence of other beings. It
seems best to begin discussion of this matter in connection with
the next objection.

*Objection 5. The argument seems to involve confusion between a priori and a
posteriori methods of demonstration.* It is important to distinguish between the kind of argument in which a conclusion is strictly deduced from premises, and the kind by which we usually establish
the existence or occurrence of any thing or state of affairs in which
we may be interested. The latter is a matter of reasonable judgement on the basis of experience, and from a strictly logical point
of view can never aspire to anything more than probability. Arguments of the former kind do yield certain conclusions, but only
at the cost of failure to establish, at least when taken by themselves, most matters of fact with which we are likely to be concerned. For at least it is not usual, when we wish to find out about
anything as a matter of scientific investigation or in the ordinary
affairs of life, for this to be merely a matter of making strict deductions from facts already known. It is uncertain which status causal
arguments of the type under discussion are presumed to have.
Are they supposed to yield the kind of certainty to be sought for in
matters of logic or mathematics? Or are they assumed rather to
supply us with merely probable conclusions on the basis of evidence in experience, which might be challenged by the adducing
of contrary evidence?[14] It may well be concluded that causal

arguments for the existence of God gain what plausibility they have through confusing these two quite distinct types of argument, and the two very different sorts of conclusion which they are capable of yielding.[15] They are arguments which rely on causality; and they are often said to establish the existence of God as a 'necessary' being as opposed to the 'contingent' beings which made up the world. And this brings out where the confusion lies; for causal arguments are essentially *a posteriori* and based upon experience, while allusion to 'necessity' indicates an appeal to what is *a priori*.

It is this underlying confusion about the type of reasoning at issue which seems particulary to have annoyed Kant about the cosmological argument. The ontological argument is frankly *a priori*, attempting as it does to establish the existence of God by sheer analysis of what is meant by 'God'; the argument from design is just as frankly an argument from experience, trying to show that there is a designer of the world from features of it analogous to the effects of human design. The cosmological argument, Kant complains, starts with what looks like an appeal to experience, but ends in a manner which shows this initial ploy to have been quite irrelevant, since the argument is really *a priori* after all. Thus this argument not only shares the defects of the ontological argument upon which it actually though surreptitiously depends; but has the additional blemish of professing 'to lead us by a new path, but after a short circuit' bringing us 'back to the very path which we had deserted at its bidding'.[16] Bertrand Russell wrote:

> It is clear that Kant is right in saying that this argument depends on the ontological argument. If the existence of the world can only be accounted for by the existence of a necessary Being, then there must be a Being whose essence involves existence, for that is what is meant by a necessary Being. But if it is possible that there should be a Being whose essence involves existence, then reason alone, without experience, can define such a Being, whose existence will follow from the ontological argument . . . The apparent greater plausibility of the cosmological as opposed to the ontological argument is therefore deceptive.[17]

It may be protested that to attribute 'necessity' as opposed to 'contingency' to God in such causal arguments is not necessarily to attribute to him the same kind of 'necessity' as is at issue in the ontological argument. Alvin Plantinga has suggested that it is worth considering, in this connection, the manner in which one may ask, of any thing or state of affairs, *why* it exists or is the case. When we have explained this in any instance, by reference to other things or states of affairs, we may press the question about those other things and states of affairs; and so on and so on. However far the question is pressed, the questioner may remain dissatisfied; and it may at length be evident that the kind of answer which he is looking for is one which is final in the sense that it leaves no question of the same sort still to be asked. 'He seems to be seeking an answer which shares with . . . analytic statement(s) the characteristic that it leaves no room for a question of the form, "Why is it that p?".'[18] One might then characterise a 'necessary' being as such that a statement referring to it may serve as a final answer in the kind of series of questions and answers just described;[19] and to call God a 'necessary being' in that case would be to bring out 'the unique role played by God's existence in the conceptual scheme of theism'.[20]

Let us concede for the purpose of the present argument that the supposition of the existence of such a being is a coherent one; and in addition that *if* God were to exist, he *would* provide an explanatory terminus of the kind described. It still remains that, if the necessity of God's existence is understood in this sense, it does not readily appear how it can form the pivot of an argument *that* God exists, either through an analysis of the concept 'God' or through attention to the nature of causality and its role in the world. *If* God exists at all, presumably he exists necessarily in this sense (not to be the kind of terminus of explanations 'Why' just described is not to be 'God' on the usual understanding of the term); but that he *would* exist 'necessarily' *in this sense*, *if* he existed at all, does not entail that he *does* exist.

Objection 6. What is invoked as causal explanation of the world cannot be referred to in the proper sense. When things and states of affairs within the world are in question, what can be argued to exist as a matter of causal probability may independently, at least in principle, be verified as existing. For example, when the existence of a planet beyond Uranus was first suspected, as accounting for anomalies observed in the orbit of Uranus, it was observation of a body of the kind and in the direction suspected which finally clinched the matter. But what would count as observation of an alleged 'first cause' of the world or 'sufficient reason' for it? As Strawson expresses Kant's conclusion on the matter, 'No object of a possible experience can answer to the ideas of an uncaused cause or a non-contingent particular existence.'[21]

God is often thought of as some kind of person; and certainly, if God were literally a 'person' in the sense of a being with physical and psychical characteristics who resided, let us suppose, somewhere beyond the farthest known galaxies, we would then have some idea of what kind of experience would supply evidence for his existence.[22] But theologians would not seem perfectly happy with such a notion of God. However, in the absence of such an account, it is doubtful how far it even makes sense to assert the existence of a being such as God is generally supposed to be.

Objection 7. The world may be simply inexplicable. In attempting to rebut Objections 1 and 2, some philosophers have argued that a cosmological or causal argument for divine existence need not envisage God as first in a series of causes of the kind with which we are acquainted within the world.[23] The world may be considered as one big object or state of affairs, if one 'lumps together' the objects and states of affairs of which it consists; and it may then be argued that, since we assume as a matter of course that other things and states of affairs have to have cause or sufficient reason for their existence, we ought if we are to be fully consistent to concede that the same applies to the thing or state of affairs which is the world as a whole.

Against this, it is retorted that it has to be shown why the universe as a whole should be ultimately explicable at all. If it is acknowledged that all the objects and states of affairs constitutive of the universe are caused in the ordinary way, is it not quite arbitrary to claim that there is needed in addition a special kind of cause for the whole *ensemble*? As Hume's Cleanthes puts it, 'Did I show you the particular causes of each individual in a collection of twenty particles of matter, I should think it very unreasonable, should you afterwards ask me, what was the cause of the whole twenty.'[24] Why should not the universe be 'de trop', as Sartre said, or 'just there and that's all', as Russell expressed it?[25] It is not as though we could argue on *inductive* grounds that the universe has to have some cause or sufficient reason outside itself; as we might do if we had had experience of many universes other than this one, and had observed all of them being created. Certainly, we know by experience that things and states of affairs within our universe are apt to be caused, to have sufficient reason; but it is difficult to see what grounds we could have for applying the principle to every thing or state of affairs within the universe, let alone for applying it to the universe as a whole. And it is hard to envisage what premisses could reasonably be advanced for a *deductive* argument yielding this conclusion.

In fact there is a very wide range of support among modern philosophers, of very different shades of opinion in other respects, for the view that the universe is simply inexplicable, and that to seek for any cause or explanation of it is consequently fruitless. There is no reason why one should not maintain that the universe is self-existent; that while things within the universe are caused, it itself is uncaused.[26] Or it may be maintained that, while the question whether there is a reason for the existence of the world makes sense, it just happens to be unanswerable, and must remain an ineradicable mystery.[27]

Objection 8. Alternatively, it may be urged that *the proposition that the universe as a whole might have an explanation has no determinate sense.* It is obvious enough that such a question as 'Where is the universe?' does not make sense, since to say *where* anything is is to assign it a location *within* the universe, in spatial relationship to other objects or aggregates which are themselves parts of the universe. The same objection could evidently be made to the question of how fast, or in what direction, the universe is moving.[28] On reflection, it may well seem that the question 'Why does the universe exist?', or 'What is the cause of the universe?', is senseless for the same kind of reason; 'why' questions about objects and states of affairs within the universe only make sense in relation to other objects and states of affairs within the universe. The question, 'Why does anything exist at all?', is 'a total question. There can be nothing not mentioned in the question to bring in to explain what is mentioned in the question . . . It is logically impossible to explain *everything*. The Principle of Sufficient Reason is demonstrably false.'[29]

Objection 9. '*Matter*', *or something like it, alone or together with something else, could be the unexplainable explanation of the things, events and states of affairs which constitute the universe as we are acquainted with it.* It has often been pointed out that, even if arguments to an uncaused cause of everything else were sound, they would not of themselves establish the existence of *God*. Reasons would have to be given in addition for thinking at least that the uncaused cause was almighty, or completely good, or in some sense personal.[30] As to the argument for a first cause as such, as Paul Edwards says, someone who believed in the eternity of atoms, or of matter in general, could quite cheerfully accept the conclusion of the argument without becoming a theist.[31]

P. F. Strawson has pointed out how, in the *Analytic* of the *Critique of Pure Reason*, Kant suggests that there might be a kind of necessity pertaining to 'permanent substances in the field of appearances' which is quite distinct from the spurious kind of necessity which is at issue in the ontological argument. A 'necessary permanence' would characterise 'particular items (substances) which can neither come into, nor go out of existence. Surely such items must possess a strong claim to the status of non-contigent existents.' In fact, Kant rejects that claim; but, according to Strawson, he gives only bad reasons for doing so. That we can think without contradiction of the non-existence of such entities does not seem a relevant objection to their possession of the sort of necessity which has just been described. Nor is it a fair objection 'that if we accepted the existence of matter as non-contingent, the free operation of the regulative principle of never-ending pursuit of explanation would receive a check. This is not so, since these non-contingent existents must be supposed to supply not the answers to our questions but their topic, the very matter of our inquiry.'[32] As an alternative to basic material entities of this kind, one might admit as the only permanent and in this sense 'necessary' existent 'the abiding spatio-temporal framework of which none of the individual constituents need be supposed to enjoy any but a contingent existence'.[33]

*   *   *

The Five Ways of Thomas Aquinas are all in some sense causal arguments for God's existence, starting from very general features of the world, and arguing to the need of another kind of being to bring such a world into existence and to keep it going.[34]

It might be claimed that these are not subject to the objections which have already been mentioned. It may be said on their behalf that their starting-points are not at all obviously unacceptable. It would be odd to deny that at least some of the things which we find about us are subject to motion or change;[35] that things are apt to be brought into existence; that they are liable to come into being and to perish; that they differ from one another in value; and that they co-operate in maintaining a fairly stable order or system.[36]

First Way.[37] (i) It is evident to our senses that some things are in motion.

    (ii) The same thing cannot be in actuality and potentiality at the same time and in the same respect.

    (iii) So it is impossible that at the same time and in the same respect a thing should be both mover and moved.

    (iv) So what is in motion must be put in motion by another.

    (v) But this cannot go back to infinity; if there were no first mover, there would be no subsequent movers.

    (vi) So it is necessary to postulate a first mover, put in motion by no other.

This Way is reminiscent of an argument advanced in the tenth book of Plato's *Laws*.[38] In Plato's time, as now, it was often maintained that the non-living or inanimate was the source or sufficient cause of the living or animate, and (interestingly) that scientific investigation tended to confirm this.[39] But Plato argued[40] that inanimate beings could not be the source of their own motion, and that the ultimate source of motion could only be what had the power of motion within itself; this he identified with 'mind' or 'soul'.[41] It is not difficult to grasp the point or to see the plausibility of this argument. Most people who are not oppressed by the bogy of scientific determinism would admit that it is up to me here and now whether I go on lying comfortably on the *chaise longue* listening to Handel, or sit up, take pen and paper, and apply myself to the difficulties surrounding the cosmological argument. If I embark on the latter course of action, I as conscious subject (or my 'mind' or 'soul' if one prefers that way of talking) am prime mover in the business. Physical objects, as contrasted with persons, have no such powers of self-determination, being subject to the laws of physics and chemistry; and non-human animals, albeit in a more complicated way, may reasonably be claimed to do whatever they do owing to the pressure of their environment upon their inheritance of instinct. One might express Plato's claim as that the workings of our own minds — our understanding, will, desire, capacity to decide, and so on — provide the best analogy by which we may grasp the nature of that which originates movement in the world.[42] Aquinas' argument as it stands[43] is more abstract, and does not directly allude to the mental attributes of the unmoved mover.

The qualification at the end of (ii) seems significant; to leave open the possibility that a thing might be in potentiality in one respect and in actuality in another respect at the same time — as Aquinas would certainly admit.[44] But at that rate, why should not a thing move or change itself, one aspect of it imparting movement or change to another? Taking motion, as Aquinas does,[45] in the very general sense of 'change', why, for example, cannot a sound jar of jam change itself, without external assistance, into a mouldy jar of jam, some chemical constituents of the sound jam acting upon others to produce a mouldy effect? Even if one grants (ii) and (iii), then, there seems no adequate reason to assent to (iv).

In fact (iv) seems to depend upon a hidden assumption, 'that rest is natural and motion is unnatural'.[46] Why should motion rather than rest need explanation? And granted that some things are moved by others, why should not others still move themselves, or just move?[47] Anthony Kenny suggests that Aquinas was deceived by the identical Latin word (*movetur*) which does duty for the two English expressions 'it moves' (in an intransitive sense) and 'it is being moved' (as by another).[48] That movement as such demanded explanation may have been a very natural assumption when there prevailed the Aristotlelian conception of motion. But it is central to the scientific conception of motion which has held sway since the seventeenth century, and which has been given overwhelming confirmation, that things will continue in uniform motion short of some particular reason why they should *not* do so.

In fact it seems that most of the difficulties of arguing to a first or uncaused cause apply equally in the case of the unmoved mover. It has just been argued in effect that there is no good reason why motion should not in some cases be a mere brute fact without explanation (cf. proposition (iv), and Objection 3). Or why should not a series of movers go back to infinity (cf. (v), and Objection 1)? Once again, there has apparently been a shift of quantifiers; as J. F. Ross says, 'there is a fallacy of logic in Aquinas' reasoning from the claim that every moved thing is in a chain of things with a first mover to the conclusion that there is one first mover of all moved things' (cf. (v) and (vi), and Objection 2).[49] Just the same objections apply if one understands 'motion' in the very general sense of 'change'.

Second Way. (i) We find an order of efficient causes in the world of sense.

    (ii) Nothing can be an efficient cause of itself, as a thing cannot be prior to itself.

    (iii) We cannot go back to infinity in the order of causes; since if there is no first cause, there will be no intermediate or proximate cause.

    (iv) So there must be a first efficient cause.

Proposition (ii) seems difficult to deny; there does seem to be a *prima facie* incoherence about a thing bringing itself into existence, or even being a causally necessary condition of its own coming into existence. At this rate, Spinoza's talk of that which is 'cause of itself'[50] appears at worst downright nonsensical, at best a confusing way of referring to what is uncaused. Objections to the other propositions have already been adduced (cf. (i) and Objection 3, (iii) and Objections 1 and 4, (iii) and (iv) and Objection 2).

Third Way. (i) We find things in the world which are possible both to be and not to be.

    (ii) Whatever is possible to be and not to be at some time is not.

    (iii) If everything were possible not to be, at some time nothing would have been in existence.

    (iv) But if at *one* time nothing existed, nothing would exist *now*; since what begins to exist does so only by virtue of something already existing.

    (v) So not all beings are possible to be and not to be; there must exist at least one necessary thing.

(vi)   But every necessary thing either has its necessity caused by another, or it does not.

(vii)   In the case of those entities whose necessity is caused by another, the series cannot go back to infinity, for reasons already given in the context of the Second Way (iii).

(viii)   So there must be some being 'having of itself its own necessity'.

It is a matter of dispute what Aquinas means by 'possible' and 'necessary' in the context of this argument.[51] On one interpretation, he means by a 'necessary' being a being the supposition of the non-existence of which is self-contradictory, and by a 'possible' being one which can coherently be supposed not to exist. On this interpretation, there is an obvious objection to (ii); why should not something, which can coherently be supposed not to exist at all, as a matter of fact have to exist at all times – as was suggested in the discussion of Objection 9? And proposition (v) is plainly liable to Objection 5. Does it make sense to claim that any matter of fact is 'necessary' in this sense? Is it not virtually an error of grammar to attribute such 'necessity', which is really a characteristic of some propositions, to things,[52] even things with such exalted status as is attributable to God?

On a second interpretation,[53] Aquinas means here by a 'necessary being' one not liable *in the course of nature* to coming into existence, or to passing out of existence or dissolution; and by a 'possible' being one which is thus liable. (The expressions ' "necessary" ' and ' "possible" ', distinguished by their inverted commas, will be used in these senses for the remainder of the discussion of this argument.) It should be noted that, in accordance with this definition, it remains possible that 'necessary' beings might be created or annihilated by divine power. On this interpretation, the objections just mentioned do not apply; that to (ii) is obviously irrelevant, and the kind of necessity attribute to analytic propositions is not at issue. But once more the fallacy of the shifted quantifier, as pointed out in Objection 2, is to be noted in the move from (vii) to (viii). Even if it be granted that every series of 'necessary' beings each of which derives its 'necessity' from other such beings must terminate in a being whose 'necessity' is not thus derivative, it does not follow that there is one and only one being from which all other 'necessary' beings derive

their 'necessity'. And the same fallacy occurs in the inference to
(iv); from (a) 'For any one "possible" thing, there was a time
when it did not exist', it does not follow that (b) 'There was a time
when no "possible" thing existed'. To get over this difficulty, it
may be suggested, on the lines of what was said in connection
with Objection 7,[54] that the totality of 'possible' things forms an
aggregate to which (a) may apply without the illegitimate inference from (a) to (b). This certainly seems plausible; surely an aggregate consisting of merely 'possible' beings, each liable to pass
out of existence, could not have persisted over an infinite time.
However, the plausibility seems to depend on the assumption
that the matter of beings which exist and are 'possible', or the
quantity of being which exists and is 'possible', is *finite*. But it has
not been shown that the amount or quantity of contigent being or
beings could not be *infinite*; and if it were, there would be no good
reasons to believe that the possibility of nothing existing would be
realised or have been realised even in an infinite time. An infinite
number of finite life-spans can stretch to infinity.[55]

The Fourth Way. (i) We find things graded in respect of goodness, truth, nobility and so on.

(ii) But things are 'more' or 'less' this and that
according as they resemble that which is
maximum in the kind.

(iii) So 'there is something which is truest, something best, something noblest, and, consequently, something which is uttermost
being'.

(iv) The maximum in any type is the cause of all
of that type.

(v) So there must be something which is cause of
the being, goodness and perfection of all
else.

The Fourth Way is apt to be depreciated even by those who believe that there is some force in the others, whether as they stand
or as modified or supplemented. With regard to (i), it may be remarked that it has been very usual, at least in the last few decades, among philosophers, to maintain that goodness, badness
and so on are rather a matter of our valuation of things, of the at-

titudes that we take up to them, than properties of the things themselves.[56] Also, things are often good under one description and bad under another,[57] as a bar of toffee may taste good and be bad for one's teeth, or a member of a university department may be good as a teacher but bad as an administrator. It may be admitted perhaps that if there is an ideal which is approached by all good things, it is plausible to call this 'God'. But in this case there seems no particular reason to maintain that 'God' actually exists.[58] And that the maximum of any class is the cause of everything in that class, as Aquinas claims (in (iv)), is demonstrably false. 'The biggest liar is not a cause of all the others.'[59]

Fifth Way. (i) We see that things in the world which lack intelligence act for an end; this is evident from their acting always, or nearly always, to get the best result.

(ii) Thus they achieve their ends not fortuitously but designedly.

(iii) But what lacks intelligence cannot move towards an end, unless directed thereto by some being with knowledge and intelligence − as an arrow shot to its mark by an archer.

(iv) Therefore some intelligent being exists which directs all natural things to their end.

In connection with this Way, and arguments to design in general,[60] it has to be asked how it is in any case that we can know when events which are apparently purposive, in working together towards an end, are actually purposed.[61] Since the appearance of Darwin's *The Origin of Species*, it has been notorious that what seems *prima facie* obviously due to intelligent design in plants and animals may at least in principle be accounted for in other ways; this contradicts (ii) and (iii). Given the amount of time for which, according to modern knowledge, the earth has been in existence and supporting life, the intricate structure which we find in organisms, and their marvellous adaptation to their environment, could have come about by a succession of random mutations followed by elimination of the unfit; as a result of prolonged study of the fossil record, we can now trace the main outline of how this must have happened. The works of man apart, organic life seems to provide the most and the clearest examples of adaptation of means to ends in the universe; if there are other instances, it seems that they can be accounted for in the same kind of way, through emergence by sheer chance, and survival due to suitability to the prevailing conditions. And the last step in the argument ((iii) to (iv)) is objectionable for a reason by now familiar to the reader (cf. Objection 2); even if there is strong evidence of design in nature apart from human contrivance, one cannot, short of the quantifier-shift so characteristic of these arguments, conclude that it is all due to just one designer.[62]

The adaptation of means to ends is certainly a sign of the operation of intelligence; though it is by no means an infallible one. Just at what point in such cases there is good reason to believe that there is intelligence at work, and why, is a difficult problem, and one to which it cannot be said that recent philosophy has provided a convincing solution.[63] But, as Kenny has pointed out, Aquinas elsewhere in his writings makes an admission which is fatal to this part of his argument. He alludes to the apparent intelligence shown by spiders and swallows, in the construction of their webs and nests, but goes on to say that we can be sure that they act by nature and not by intelligence, since they always act in the same manner.[64] In contrast with human builders of houses, they cannot build in a variety of ways, or adapt the way in which they build to particular circumstances. In accordance with this principle, which seems convincing enough at first sight at least, it is only what one might call irregular adaptive behaviour, and not regular adaptive behaviour, which is a reliable indication of the operation of intelligence. But we have no evidence that anything exists, other than human beings, which displays irregular adaptive behaviour, and must in consequence be intelligent on the given assumption.[65]

It has been argued by William H. Baumer that all Five Ways depend surreptitiously on the ontological argument, in the manner claimed by Kant to be characteristic of cosmological arguments. The essence of an ontological argument is to show 'that the understanding of what a thing is is *eo ipso* an understanding that it is'.[66] 'To think of an absolutely necessary being which does not exist is to think of an absolutely necessary being which is not even necessary, much less absolutely so'; just as 'to think of a most real being which does not exist is to think of a most real being which is not even real, much less most so'.[67] So much for the Third Way. The first two Ways are supposed to establish the existence of 'a first actuality', the Fourth that of something which is 'most being', the Fifth that of 'a first intelligence'. 'A first actuality which does not exist is not an actuality; a most being which is not is not even a being, and a non-existent intelligence is not a first one'.[68] One might put it that those who would contest these suggestions are involved in the absurdity with which Anselm rightly charged the fool, of claiming of that which existed supremely that it did not exist at all.[69]

It may be concluded from what has been said that the Five Ways are liable not only to many of the same objections as the other kinds of causal argument for God's existence which we have considered, but to other objections which apply peculiarly to themselves.

3 On Knowledge and Experience

An excursion into the theory of knowledge may seem quite out of place within a treatment of the cosmological argument. But I am convinced that this is not so, for reasons which will appear in what follows, and may be briefly summarised immediately. According to one conception of knowledge, what is primarily constitutive of it is·experience; according to another, it consists of true belief backed up by reasons. (The two conceptions are set out by Plato in the *Theaetetus*, and are apparently both rejected by him.)[1] From the former conception of the nature of knowledge, the impossibility of knowing that God exists almost immediately follows; since God is not generally supposed to be an actual or conceivable object of 'experience' in any of the common senses of the term. From the latter conception, it by no means so obviously follows; and indeed this conception is very suggestive of ways in which claims to knowledge of God's existence, particularly those depending to a greater or lesser extent on cosmological arguments, might be validated. It is therefore relevant to our main topic to consider which, if either, of these two conceptions of the nature and the scope of human knowledge is liable to be correct.

It is clear that there is a certain *prima facie* plausibility in the view that it is experience which makes the difference between knowledge on the one hand, and ignorance or mere belief on the other. I may for example not be aware at all that there is a blackbird feeding in my garden, or believe it with no great degree of confidence when informed to that effect by a child of five; but when I have seen the bird myself, I may reasonably be claimed to have progressed from ignorance or mere belief about the matter to knowledge. In this case, as in innumerable similar ones, it is through experience that I am more or less directly acquainted[2]

24

with a state of affairs about which I may previously have been entirely ignorant, or come to some belief on the testimony of others; and after the experience and as a result of it I may reasonably be said to have knowledge of that state of affairs.

In this case and in similar ones, again, it seems at least at first sight that that which is the object of my experience, that which I see or hear, is identical with that which I come to know. But in other cases of what would at least normally and in most circumstances be counted as coming to know something, that which I come to know, and the object of the experience which is the occasion of my coming to know it, are two very different things. Three types of example illustrate the point with special vividness – knowledge of the past, knowledge of the thoughts and feelings of other persons, and knowledge of the fundamental particles of nuclear physics. As a schoolboy, I may come to know that King Charles I was beheaded, as a result either of hearing the words of one of my teachers, or of seeing what is written in the pages of a book; but the fact of his being beheaded on the one hand, and the existence of the marks on paper or the occurrence of the sounds which are the basis in my experience for my coming to know that fact on the other, are obviously very different things. The same seems to apply to my knowledge of the fact that you have a severe headache, or are worried about the late return of your niece from the cinema; I can know what you are feeling or thinking on the basis of the overt behaviour of yours that I see or the words of yours that I hear, but the behaviour and speech are one thing, your feeling or thought (as would generally be admitted)[3] another. Again, a nuclear physicist may come to know of the existence of a new kind of fundamental particle not because he has observed it or could possibly observe it, but because observations may be made and experimental results obtained which are best *explained* on the hypothesis that such particles exist.[4]

Now what is crucial for our purposes here about these three examples of coming to know is that what comes to be *known* is beyond anything which is or apparently could be *observed*. I do not perceive the historical event, or your mental state as such, or the fundamental particles; however, I do perceive that of which the real occurrence of that historical event, or your really being in that particular mental state, or the real existence of particles of that particular kind, seem, in conjunction with the rest of what

I perceive and believe, to be the best available explanation. Other mental performances, over and above what can be regarded even in the broadest sense as 'sensation', 'perception' or 'observation', seem to be involved in these cases of coming to know. Of what nature are these? At least two kinds of performance seem necessarily and indispensably involved. It is one thing to think up a possible explanation of an observation; it is another to suppose that the possible explanation is correct. I may entertain the supposition that you have a headache, or that you are worried about your niece, from your restlessness or your morose expression. But there may well be other plausible explanations; for example, that you are irritated by my presence, or preoccupied by the size of the overdraft on your bank account. However, it may be that the evidence available to me will to all intents and purposes clinch the matter; for example, if you speak to me of your headache or your concern for your niece, and I have no reason to suppose that you have any motive for deceiving me about the matter, out of politeness, or resentment at my interference, or a compulsive disposition to tell lies.

Evidently there are many respects in which our acquisition of knowledge of the past, and of the theoretical entities postulated by physicists, differ from one another and from that of the thoughts, feelings and sensations of other persons. But at least they seem to have in common with one another the features I mentioned in the last paragraph. In the case of inquiry into the remote past, one may think of a possible explanation, for example of a puzzling lacuna in a document or of stylistic features in a monument which one would not generally associate with the period to which it is assigned; and find that this explanation tends to be confirmed as in all probability the right one, or impugned as almost certainly the wrong one, when one attends to other available evidence bearing on the matter. It is just the same with the scientific example. The well-informed student of any branch of science knows what observations and experimental results tend to support the prevailing theories, and to count against obvious alternatives.[5]

It may be objected that it is widely maintained that to speak of the thoughts and feelings of persons is nothing else than to speak conveniently of the observable behaviour they do display or would display in appropriate circumstances; and that talk of fundamental particles is similarly merely a useful way of alluding to a vast assemblage of observations and experimental results. But to apply the moral to a statement about the remote past would be paradoxical indeed. Few claims could run more contrary to our intuitions than that the statement, 'Charles I was beheaded in 1649', made in 1980, *means* that in the latter year certain noises will, or would in certain circumstances, be made by professional historians, and that certain patterns of print will be found by the curious on certain pages of books. In this case it seems as obvious as could well be that the *fact* which is *meant* by the statement in question is distinct from the *perceptual evidence* which anyone may *now* have for the truth of that statement. (The same would evidently apply in the case of an inquiry held by a court as to whether someone had poisoned his mother-in-law; the object of the exercise would be to determine on the basis of evidence available *here and now* whether the defendant had administered the poison *there and then*. Hardly anyone, except perhaps an epistemologist determined to defend his theory at all costs, would maintain that the matter of fact which the court was trying to ascertain was identical with the evidence available in principle to them for ascertaining it.)[6] But if it is so obvious that, in the case of statements about the past, the meaning of what is stated goes far beyond what could conceivably be perceived by the person who makes the statement, for all that it may be supported or impugned by what *is* available to perception, why should not the same be admitted in the case of statements about other minds and the particles of nuclear physics? Do not the 'behaviourist' and 'operationist' accounts of these statements presuppose an assumption clearly falsified in the historical case, that what is knowable cannot be other than what is or could be perceived?

I have distinguished two sorts of mental operation, over and above perception, characteristically involved in coming to know. As well as attention to evidence available in experience, there is envisagement of possible explanations for this, and fixing upon the one of these explanations which seems best to fit the evidence. Let us say that a person is *attentive* to the degree that he has a disposition to perform this first type of mental operation, and that he is *intelligent* and *reasonable* respectively to the degree that he has a disposition to perform the second and third.[7] It is to be noted that intelligence and reasonableness as thus conceived are largely a matter of asking and answering questions, and that there are salient differences between the sorts of questions pertaining to each type of mental operation. The asking and answering of questions which are a matter of reasonableness presuppose the asking and answering of questions which are a matter of intelligence; I must be in possession of a hypothesis, envisage a possibility, before I am in a position to ask whether the hypothesis is true, the possibility actually so. Another difference is that questions for reasonableness, unlike questions for intelligence, can be answered 'Yes' and 'No'. I cannot say 'What is this? Yes or No?', as I can say, 'Is this a goldcrest? Yes or no?' I cannot answer 'Yes' or 'No' to the questions, 'How did Charles I meet his death?', or 'What is the explanation of my friend's fidgeting and abstracted manner?' But once the possibility has occurred to me that Charles I was beheaded, or that my friend is worried about his niece, I may be in a position to answer 'Yes' or 'No' the ensuing question of whether either of these possibilities is actually so. Suppose again that I am a student of physics, confronted with the results of the experiment which led to the supersession of Thomson's account of the constitution of the atom by that of Rutherford. If I am asked, 'What could be the explanation of these results?', or 'How could this be accounted for?', it makes no sense for me to answer 'Yes' or 'No'. But if Rutherford's account and Thomson's occur to me as possible explanations, I can ask whether each of them is probably or certainly so, and answer 'Yes' or 'No' on the basis of the evidence provided by the experiment.[8]

It might still be objected that examples of these three kinds of what, on the usual conceptions of knowledge, we can be said to know, are after all not really 'knowledge', just because they go beyond in the manner described what we can or conceivably could perceive. But it may be asked what good reason there could be for believing that *real* knowledge must be of that which is or may be perceived (at least in the case of contingent propositions), when it is so easy to show that so many cases of what usually counts as knowledge go beyond what may be perceived. It seems, from all the cases considered so far in this section, that perception is a characteristic *part of* coming to know; and this makes it easy to understand why there should arise a prejudice to the effect that all objects of knowledge must be actual or at least potential objects of perception. But even those cases where they are so conform very well to the account of coming to know derived from our other type of example, where the known is what is intelligently conceived and reasonably affirmed on the basis of perception. After all, I can properly be said to know afterwards that there was a black-bird in my garden at the time at which I perceived it, even when I no longer perceive it; in this case my recollected perception provides a basis for my reasonable judgement that there was a blackbird there at that time.

Someone might raise the following objection. 'But knowledge of a proposition implies that that proposition is true. How can you be sure that your admittedly reasonable judgement on the basis of intelligent assessment of the available evidence in perception is not all the same false?' I cannot be perfectly sure. It is possible that my sensation as though of a blackbird may be a hallucina-tion, or that I may, owing to a trick of the light, mistake a starling or a thrush or even a piece of dirty rag for a blackbird. I might even in future find evidence mounting up in favour of one of these suppositions, which would explain my having enjoyed experience as though of a blackbird without a real blackbird having been where I judged it to be as a result of the experience. If it *were* thus to mount up, I would have to admit that my previous claim to knowledge on the matter, however *reasonable* at the time, was *mistaken*; thus my present claim to knowledge entails that evi-dence would *not* tend to mount up in such a way if I *were* seriously to investigate it. On most topics about which we claim knowl-edge, attentiveness might conceivably turn up fresh evidence, and intelligence envisage new possibilities, which would make a different judgement than our usual one as to what is so more reasonable. For example, on the basis of observations made and experiments performed up to late in the eighteenth century, it was very reasonable to suppose that metals lost a substance which was called phlogiston when subject to tarnishing or combustion. On the basis of evidence available since that time, it is now far more reasonable to suppose that they become combined in these circumstances with a substance which we call oxygen. Again, that the stars were fixed in a hollow crystal sphere which whirled around a stable earth was once about the most reasonable ex-planation of their observed motions; that there were not violent winds blowing perpetually in the same direction, and that the oceans did not incontinently pour over the land, apparently was evidence enough that the alternative possibility, that it was the earth which was spinning, was incorrect. Now that much more evidence has been attended to, and many more explanations en-visaged, than when that theory was in vogue, it is incomparably more reasonable to hold the latter view of the matter than the former. We can properly *claim* to know when we have good reason in experience to support our belief, *on the assumption* that subsequent experience will not tend to build up in such a way as to indicate that the belief is false; even though it may be that we or others ultimately have good reason to reject our claim to knowledge as mistaken. However, it is worth noting that our judgements about what is the case and can be observed in the world immediately about us, where no matter of scientific theory is presupposed, are not on the whole much at risk in the manner just illustrated. A man who is convinced, in a good light, that he sees a blackbird at close quarters, when he is aware of the difference between a bird of that species and a starling or a jackdaw, does not usually find good reason to revise his opinion.[9]

One may be thoroughly attentive to evidence, intelligent in envisaging possibilities, and reasonable in judgement, without judging truly and thus knowing; and one may happen to judge truly while being very little attentive, intelligent or reasonable. Yet it remains the case that true judgement is, and cannot but be, the term towards which the exercise of these mental capacities tends to approach. This seems to be confirmed by every example, whether in ordinary life or in matters of scientific or scholarly inquiry, where we find that we have now attained the truth, or at least have come closer to the truth, on a matter about which we had previously been ignorant or in error. There is not a merely contingent connection between tending towards knowledge of the truth on the one hand, and conceiving intelligently and affirming reasonably on the basis of attention to as much of the relevant evidence as is available on the other. An example may suggest the reasonableness of this claim, which I will later try to support with more cogent arguments. In a murder investigation, the most ignorant and prejudiced person may hit by accident upon the correct verdict; while the most conscientious conceivable court of law, which goes over the evidence and envisages and tests explanations for it in the most thorough and painstaking way, may yet fail to do so. But it would obviously be wrong to infer from this that one might just as well take the word of the first person one happens to meet with an opinion on the matter as incur all the trouble and expense of a trial. And to say that the opinion of an ignorant and prejudiced person, where it differed from the conclusions of the conscientious court, had turned out to be right after all, would be to imply that an even wider consideration of relevant evidence, an even more extensive envisagement of possibilities — including perhaps those rejected on evidence previously amassed — and an even more rigorous exercise of judgement, than had been achieved by the court, had confirmed that person's opinion. Almost any detective story will serve as illustration of what it is to reject one opinion which was reasonable so far as it went, and reasonably to come to another, on matters of this kind.

But there is no need to rely on a mere citing of illustrative examples to make this point. The fact is that the contradictory of the proposition, that one tends to get at the truth by exercise of the capacities that we have called attentiveness, intelligence and reasonableness, is self-destructive. Suppose someone denies that one or all of these capacities are characteristically employed in coming to know the truth. Has he attended to the evidence bearing on the matter? Has he envisaged ways in which that evidence might be accounted for? Has he formed his judgement on the matter in accordance with its support by the evidence in opposition to possible alternatives? If he (or perhaps the authority on which he relies) has omitted any one of these steps, he is not to be taken seriously; what general form could the vindication of any thesis take other than this one, if it were even to count as the vindication of a thesis? If he has gone through them all, and admits their relevance to the establishment of his case, then he has exercised in order to come to know the truth in this case the very capacities whose relevance to coming to know the truth he is denying.[10]

It is important to notice that to say that we can come to make true statements for good reason is as much as to say that we can get to know the world as it really is. 'The world is everything that is the case';[11] and by exercising our capacities of attentiveness, intelligence and reasonableness, we can make true statements about what is the case, and hence come to know the world. The world consists of facts, as Wittgenstein said;[12] facts are what true statements state, as J. L. Austin said; and so if we can come to make true statements for good reason we can *ipso facto* obtain knowledge of the real world. Descartes' question of how one can break out of the circle of one's thoughts or sensations to attain knowledge of a real external world is thus wrongly posed.[13] It may well be the case that one's evidence for how things are in the world always terminates in some experience within oneself;[14] but

I have already pointed out the fallacy involved in failing to distinguish between a fact known by means of evidence on the one hand — intelligently conceived and reasonably affirmed on the basis of that evidence — and the evidence by means of which that fact is known on the other.

The currently more fashionable conundrum, of how we can break out of the-world-for-our-society to knowledge of the real world as it exists independently of us and our society, is wrongly posed for just the same reason.[15] To speak of a world 'for me' or 'for my society' entails the possibility of what P. F. Strawson calls a 'corrected viewpoint'[16] to give significance to the implied contrast. The world 'for' or 'of' any particular person is the totality of things and states of affairs which he believes to exist or to obtain, by a compound of the result of the exercise of his own cognitive faculties with what he has taken over from his community in the process of learning to speak its language, being subjected to its educational system, and so on. The real world as opposed to the world-for-him is what he *would* tend to come to know so far as he exercised his cognitive faculties to an indefinite extent; and the same applies, *mutatis mutandis*, to the world 'for' and 'of' each society.

It is worth pointing out that on this account the worlds 'for' and 'of' different persons and societies will in a sense be *parts of* the real world; to get to know them, one must attend to the relevant evidence (in their noises and gestures, in the documents and monuments which they have left, and so on); one must envisage a sufficiently wide range of possibilities of what their conceptions of and beliefs about things might be; and one must provisionally judge that account to be correct which consorts best with the evidence. What is the case about other minds, or indeed about our own, is known as a particular item of what is known in general, and as distinct from the rest of what is known. That there is a real world, and not merely a series of perceptions or sensations which is myself alone, or myself in my immediate environment, follows directly from the facts that true judgements are possible, and that the real world is nothing other than what such true judgements are about. My mind, my body and my immediate environment, are only *among* the range of things about which I can come to make such true judgements.

The reader may still object that all the same the *real* world, consisting of 'things in themselves', or things as they actually are apart from the perceptions, conceptions and interests of human individuals or societies, might somehow after all be other than what we tend intelligently to conceive and reasonably to affirm as a result of persistent questioning of our experience. But short of such a potential relation to our conception and affirmation, notions like 'real', 'thing' and 'world' are themselves bereft of significance. We cannot coherently suppose that things as they are in themselves might really bear no such relation; therefore we *can* know that they *must* have such a relation. If 'reality', 'things in themselves', or 'the actual world', are not to be known as a result of attentive, intelligent and reasonable correction of our present judgements, they are nothing. For notions like 'error' or 'mere appearance' to get any purchase, one must be able in principle to spell out how it is possible to correct such error or pierce through such appearance. The mistake underlying the contradictory view is confusion of the true proposition that most beliefs which human beings arrive at are conceivably liable to correction, with the falsehood that knowledge of anything as it really is, and would have been apart from our knowledge of it, is absolutely beyond our grasp.

In cases of arguments supposed to establish some matter of fact, it is often asked whether the reasoning involved is deductive or inductive. This alternative is apt to be very misleading, owing to the ambiguity of the term 'induction'. This may be taken in a narrow sense, as amounting only to what one might call 'simple induction'. Here one infers from a number of cases where things of type x have turned out to have property y, when there are no known instances of such things failing to have that property, that some other x has that property, or that all xs have that property.[17] Let us say, for example, that by a 'raven' I mean a bird which is uniformly black, has a wedge-shaped tail, is twenty-five inches long (give or take a couple of inches) when fully grown, utters a deep croak, and is a descendant of closely similar birds. Having observed, or knowing that others have observed, a number of birds of this description, I see a large black bird about twenty-five inches long, and I infer 'This is a raven', implying that it will turn out to have a wedge-shaped tail, utter a deep croak, and be descended from closely similar birds. Of course it has been notorious, since Hume drew attention to what is called 'the problem of induction',[18] that so far as strict logic is concerned, there is no reason why a bird which *looks* in all respects like ravens have always looked should not utter shrill screams, and have emerged from an egg laid by a creature in all other respects like a scorpion. It is of no use protesting that such cases have never occurred in the past, since there is no reason, so far as logic strictly speaking is concerned, why the future should be like the past. That it will be so is just the same kind of assumption as that those birds which have one set of characteristics of ravens always have the rest.

But in any case, if deductive reasoning is quite inadequate by itself for acquiring much knowledge which is worth the name, in science or in the ordinary affairs of life, it is hardly more satisfactory when eked out by simple induction. The point may conveniently be illustrated by reference to the three classes of states of affairs already discussed in connection with the problem of the relation of knowledge to experience. In inferring what you are thinking and feeling from the gestures which you make and the noises which you emit, I cannot rely upon the fact that I have always observed that such thoughts and feelings were enjoyed by you and other people when you produced such gestures and noises, since I could not possibly have made any such observation. And even if it were argued, as it has been and might still be at a pinch,[19] that I extrapolate from my own case, the same principle could hardly be applied to nuclear physics. Physicists often seem perfectly justified in saying that a streak on a photographic plate was caused by the passage of an alpha particle; but this is not because whenever they or their colleagues have looked carefully at such tracks being made, they have observed alpha particles making them.

It may be protested that 'induction' is far more inclusive than what I have called 'simple induction'. But the trouble then is that it seems *too* inclusive, and to cover all types of reasoning involved in finding out about matters of fact which cannot be reduced to deduction.[20] In that case, the apparently informative principle that all valid reasoning involved in establishing matters of fact is either deductive or inductive, turns out to amount to no more than the empty tautology that such reasoning either is deductive or is not.

However, if the reasoning involved in establishing matters of fact is to be understood as a matter of persistent application of the three types of mental operation already described, it is easy to see the scope and limits of deduction, and to articulate and justify so far as is possible the types of reasoning generally referred to as 'inductive'. Deductive reasoning is of particular importance with respect to the operation of reasonableness, though it is by no means exhaustive of it. Once I have, by the operation of intelligence, arrived at one or more explanations of a set of observed data, I have to *deduce* the consequences of these explanations, in order to *test* them against more observations. But since there is likely to be a gap between any deduction from an explanation of a set of data, and any record of an observation of such data, the operation of reasonableness cannot be reduced to such deduction; there remains the matching of what has been deduced with the observations. It is one thing to work out theoretically what would be the effect of a particle travelling in the neighbourhood of the atoms of a gas; it is another thing to claim that a streak observed on a photograph is a record of such an effect. Similarly, it is one thing to work out, from a general notion of what one's friend thinks and feels, what he might mean to say in a situation; it is another thing to judge that a particular complex of observable sounds and gestures express that meaning.

'Simple induction' is just one kind of application of intelligence and reasonableness to experience.[21] Let us suppose that I conclude, as a result of a series of observations as of a bird of a certain size and colour, that I have seen a raven. Let us suppose in addition that I am a seasoned ornithologist, that the visibility is good, that I am not drugged or drunk or habitually subject to hallucinations, and that the habitat is one appropriate for ravens – not, for example, a psychology laboratory where *trompe l'œil* devices might be expected, real ravens not. In this case, it will be more reasonable to suppose that the explanation for my having visual experiences as of a raven will be the actual presence of a raven, rather than that I am the victim of a delusion due to the machinations of my enemies or the diseased state of my brain. Of all the possible explanations which a fertile intelligence might concoct for my experience, that I have seen a raven, in the sense which entails that an actual raven has been before my eyes, is the most reasonable, given all the circumstances.

It may be concluded that our general account of the mental operations involved in getting to know the truth about things will account for 'simple induction' as well as for 'induction' of the more obscure kinds; and that these operations include 'deduction' as one essential component. One of the most enlightening accounts of the kind of reasoning necessary, apart from deduction, for achieving results in scientific or historical investigation, has been provided by C. S. Peirce. As Peirce sees it, the following is an example of what he calls an 'abductive' inference:

> A surprising fact, B, is observed.
> But if A were true, B would be a matter of course.
> Therefore, there is reason to suspect that A is true.[22]

It may easily be seen that 'abductive inference' is a matter of what is described here as reasonable judgement based on attentiveness and intelligence; one has to attend to the surprising fact, intelligently conceive a range of possible explanations for it, and reasonably settle for the one which best explains the fact and the rest of the relevant evidence.

One of the most important corollaries of the account of knowledge which I have been sketching is the principle of sufficient reason. According to that account, a known fact commends itself as such by being sufficient reason both for states of affairs of which one's experience gives one *prima facie* evidence (as my experience as of oranges in front of me on the table gives me *prima facie* evidence that there are in fact oranges in front of me on the table), and other known facts. As Hume in effect pointed out, apart from the assumption that states of affairs are related to each other and to our knowledge in this kind of way, some providing sufficient reason for the existence and occurrence of others, we would have no means of extending our knowledge beyond the content of our present experience and our memory of past experience.[23] (The conviction that we could extend it even so far is probably unduly sanguine.[24]) When we run into an apparently unexplained 'fact' in the course of experience or inquiry, we assume that the anomaly will be eliminated by further experience or inquiry; and our very confidence in our capacity to inquire successfully into how things are or have been in the world presupposes that we do so. For once we allow exceptions anywhere, why not allow them everywhere? Why take the data which are the starting-points for scientific and historical investigation as evidence *for* anything at all, when *ex hypothesi* they could just have been present to our senses without explanation?[25]

It should be noted that, whatever Hume and some of his successors may have inferred from it,[26] it does not appear that the principle of sufficient reason in this sense leads necessarily to determinism. To explain why something happened or was done is by no means necessarily to explain why it could not but have happened or been done. I may have motives for going to the Senior Common Room today to have lunch, and other motives for eating a sandwich in my office instead; whichever I choose to do, my action will be explicable, will have sufficient reason, in my own state and in the state of my environment at the time. It may be objected that the stronger motives will prevail, but the claim is an ambiguous one. One may define as 'the stronger set of motives' any set on which a person happens to act in a case of conflict; but then it is a mere tautology to claim that one always acts on the stronger motives. If, on the other hand, it is implied that in every case of the resolution of such conflict there is always something which makes the agent unable in the last analysis to act in any way other than he does, then this presupposes determinism, and cannot be used as an argument for it. If a historian is trying to explain why Caesar crossed the Rubicon, he will set out to show that Caesar was able to cross it and had motives for crossing it when he did. He need not affect to demonstrate how Caesar could not but have crossed the Rubicon just then. Notoriously, he had weighty reasons for not doing so; had he refrained, historians would have been able to explain the fact just as well as they can the fact of his crossing.

The point can also be made by appeal to a very different kind of example. In giving an explanation of the evolution of, say, the giraffe, a zoologist would have to describe conditions likely to have obtained which were such that animals of this sort *could have* evolved; it would be absurd for him to purport to specify conditions in which they *could not but have* evolved. And the account given by physicists of radioactive decay seems to have a similar lack of determinateness, at least as applied to individual atoms. If it is known that the half-life of a radioactive element is X years, it can be inferred that half the atoms in a sufficiently large sample will have turned into atoms of the next element in the radioactive series in X years; but in the case of any particular atom, so far as is yet known, it is really possible that it will change in the next second, or that it will not do so for X million years. It may be protested that explanations of these kinds are incomplete; but we have no way of knowing for sure that explanations which are complete in the corresponding sense are available in matters of these kinds. And it may well be felt that the kind of explanation which we accept as a matter of course for human action, and the fact that the (virtually) inexorable laws of the physics of large bodies can very well be explained on the basis of merely statistical laws governing fundamental particles, suggests that it is not possible.

Let us call the states of affairs which make possible in this sense, but do not necessitate, such events as my going to lunch, Caesar's crossing of the Rubicon, the evolution of the giraffe, and the transmutation of any atom of a radioactive element, *enabling conditions* of these events. One might then put it that the principle of sufficient reason, so far as it is implicit in the account of our knowledge of the world which I have sketched, commits one to the view that contingent things, events and states of affairs must have enabling conditions, but not necessarily the *causally necessitating conditions* on which determinists insist.

Another corollary of the account of knowledge which I have outlined above is that one may make statements whose contradictories are *self-destructive* without being *self-contradictory* – a distinction which will prove of some importance in what follows. A self-destructive statement is one which entails that the procedures necessarily involved in making it for good reason have not taken place. The statement, whether made by Smith or anyone else, that Smith never speaks the truth, or never has good reason for saying what he says, is not self-contradictory. Made about Smith by another than Smith, it is not self-destructive. But made by Smith about himself, it *is* self-destructive. Similarly, it is self-destructive for Smith to argue for a proposition which entails that he is not an arguer, or, as Descartes noted, to think that he is not a thinker.[27] These cases are obvious enough; in others, the self-destructiveness of what someone says may be concealed. For example, if it can be inferred from the propositions constitutive of behaviourism that no one, not even the behaviourist, says what he says because there is good reason for him to do so, then behaviourism is self-destructive in a manner which may not be obvious to everyone.[28]

The contradictories of those propositions which are self-destructive in the manner which I have tried to illustrate are in a sense at once synthetic and *a priori*. They are not *a priori* in the sense of being self-evident, or such that it is not possible sincerely to deny them. They are not analytic, since they are not true simply by virtue of the meanings of the terms employed in making them, and their negations are not self-contradictory. But they *are a priori* in the sense that all our knowledge of and inquiry into what is so presuppose them, and in that we do not learn them by 'experience', at least in quite the usual sense of the term. It is not possible to show by experience, after all, that we are able to come to know by means of our experience of the nature and existence of things which are and are what they are independently of and prior to our experience.

It may easily be seen that the 'hypothetico-deductive method' constitutive of science is nothing other than a thorough application of the mental processes which are necessarily involved in coming to know. To form a 'hypothesis' to account for some puzzling phenomenon is nothing else than to exercise the capacity of intelligence with respect to it; to deduce its consequences, and to test it by comparing these with relevant observations or experimental results, is nothing else than to exercise the capacity of reasonableness. And to ask appropriate questions in the first place, and ultimately to evaluate the various possible answers to them, one must be attentive to experience. If this is the case, appropriate methods in science are not simply to be taken on trust on the authority of trained groups of specialists;[29] they can be shown, by the very nature of knowledge, to be the appropriate methods of coming to know and getting at the truth on the matters with which they deal. The layman is right to accept the authority of the scientist or other expert *because*, and *in so far as*, the expert and the members of the specialty to which he belongs have had and used the opportunity to be especially attentive, intelligent and reasonable in the fields which are their particular concern.[30]

The verification principle of the logical positivists seems to be self-destructive in the manner which I have already described; since there is no course of sense-experience in which one could conceivably tend to verify or falsify the meaningful non-analytic proposition that all meaningful non-analytical propositions tend to be verified or falsified by sense-experience.[31] But if the account which I have given is on the right lines, one can see why the verification principle should have commended itself to some philosophers, and why something like it may remain as a useful rule of thumb in most investigations into what is so. (This is what it seems to have amounted to in the form in which Wittgenstein is supposed first to have pronounced it.[32]) If one is to arrive at a reasonable judgement on any matter, on the principles we have outlined, one will have to have some notion of what kind of experience would tend to confirm the judgement, what to impugn it; as of course is entailed by the verification principle.

According to Karl Popper, who developed his views in conscious opposition to the logical positivists, statements are scientific so far as they are falsifiable in observation or experiment, but are corroborated in virtue of survival of attempts to falsify them.[33] There is an awkward question about the status of this principle itself. Popper writes that 'it is through the falsification of our suppositions that we actually get in touch with reality'.[34] Could *this* supposition conceivably be falsified, or could it not? It is difficult to see how one would go about trying to falsify it. But if it could not, what grounds are there, other than caprice, convention or deference to authority, for holding it? It is all very well saying that it is open to critical discussion;[35] but unless the nature and limits of such discussion are made more specific, a flat-earther might say just the same about his own position. I suggest that Popper's position, or a version of it, is falsifiable in one sense, but not in another; and why this is so may be inferred from the account of knowledge which I have sketched. There are alternative positions which might be argued; but they turn out invariably to be self-destructive, if Popper's maxim is interpreted as a corollary of the position I have set out. It is self-destructive to deny that we tend by and large to get at the truth by making sure that we have good reason for what we say. And to have such good reason can only be to have attended to the relevant evidence, to have envisaged a range of possible explanations, and to have preferred the judgement we make as the possibility which accounts most adequately for the evidence. The business of eliminating alternative accounts, and leaving the best available approximation to truth as survivor, is what Popper has been most concerned to emphasise in his work.

While the logical positivists dismissed metaphysics as due merely to the abuse of language, Popper regards it as consisting of untestable statements which may have the merit of being able to be refined into, or otherwise give rise to, statements which are testable and so genuinely scientific.[36] But there is another kind of 'metaphysics' which might be developed through the working-out of the implications of Popper's position; consisting of what can be inferred from the fact that the world is such, and in an important sense cannot but be such, as to be able to be known progressively through the method of the propounding and testing of hypotheses. This thesis, and what may be inferred from it, is evidently not 'falsifiable' in the sense that one could specify what course of observations or what experimental results would be inconsistent with it; since one cannot by observation and experiment test the thesis that the real world is to be known through the process of testing one's theses by observation and experiment. But it *is* testable, I believe, in that to state its contradictory may be shown to have implications which are self-destructive. From the fact that Popper uses 'metaphysics' and cognate terms in a sense different from that suggested here, it does not follow that such a view would not amount to a consistent development of his position.

It seems to me that the usual criticisms of Popper — for example those made by Kuhn and Feyerabend — either can be rebutted, or are not applicable to the matter at issue here. Mostly these criticisms fasten especially on the principle of falsifiability. In terms of the terminology employed here, they seem to bring to Popper's account the same kind of objection as Popper brings to the empiricists' account of the operation of intelligence — that it cannot be reduced to rule. Just as there is a gap between any set of observations one may make and any hypothesis which one might propose to account for them, so there is a gap between any deductions which can validly be made from a hypothesis and the observations which might tend to falsify or corroborate it. The alleged failure of both Popperian and empiricist accounts of how truth is to be arrived at has led some to suppose that one had better, at least in science, give up the ideal of truth, and submit (as Kuhn recommends) to such dogmatic definitions as may be propounded by the relevant professional authorities; or prefer (in the manner of Feyerabend) whatever account seems most liberating or aesthetically attractive.[37]

But even if Popper's actual account of the operation of reasonableness were not perfectly satisfactory, it would not follow that reasonableness as more accurately delineated, along with attentiveness and intelligence, was not the right means of approaching towards the truth about the world. And the odd thing about the criticisms, as they have actually been set out by Kuhn and Feyerabend, is that they seem to presuppose in application to historical inquiry a conception of truth and how it is to be arrived at whose application to science they reject. In defence of their own views, they employ historical arguments about how observations have in fact been made, how theories have been propounded and defended and so forth, in which they by no means merely defer to established authority, or commend what they say merely as pleasing or liberating. On the contrary, they draw the attention of their readers to the available evidence; they set out their own accounts of what conduces to acknowledged scientific progress alongside the accounts of Popper and their other opponents; and they submit their own as likely to be correct on the ground that they square better with the evidence than do those of their rivals.[38] They thus seem to corroborate what they say in properly Popperian fashion, by refuting the opposition. However, they do seem to have made a case against the principle of falsification being quite so satisfactory or inclusive an articulation of the operation of reasonableness as Popper appears to claim. At least in the short run, judging from the history of science, it may turn out to be the best policy to retain a theory in the face of *prima facie* anomalies,[39] or to elaborate it in order to accommodate them, rather than to reject it outright.

I have been at pains to emphasise that the fact which a true statement states, and the grounds in experience upon the basis of which that statement is justifiably made, are characteristically distinct from one another. (They are identical only in those cases where one judges that one is having a certain experience.[40]) If knowledge is justified true belief, its truth has one kind of relation to the fact by virtue of which it is true, another kind of relation to the evidence which justifies it. I think that it is largely inadvertence to the distinction between these two kinds of relation which leads people to abandon the correspondence theory of truth and espouse the coherence theory. The reason for this is as follows. Whether our statements are likely to be true, to correspond with the facts, does depend on experience; since attention to experience is on the whole a crucial and indispensable component in our coming to know what is so. But much more is, at least at first sight, implied by most of our statements than that certain experiences have been, are, or will be enjoyed in the appropriate circumstances by ourselves or other persons. Typically, our statements involve intellectual constructions which, if the statements are to be true, must be coherent within themselves and with other similar intellectual constructions. For me to speak the truth about what lies beyond my experience, my discourse must be coherent. As a fair proportion of my statements go beyond my experience, and statements have on the whole to be coherent with one another if they are to be accepted as true, it is apt to be concluded that truth is a matter of the coherence of propositions with one another rather than of correspondence between them and facts.

But what leads to the coherence theory of truth is a very natural misunderstanding of what it is for a statement to correspond with a fact, which depends in its turn on a confusion between the two types of relation which I mentioned, between a statement and the fact which it states on the one hand, and the statement and the evidence for the fact which it states on the other. Let us say that a true statement corresponds$_1$ with the fact which makes it true, and, when made for good reason, corresponds$_2$ with the evidence used to support it. To be worthy of acceptance as corresponding$_1$ with a fact, a statement must be actually or potentially coherent with a whole system of statements some of which correspond$_2$, and very few of which are in *prima facie* conflict, with evidence available in experience. The coherence theory of truth stands as a useful corrective to that kind of correspondence theory which envisages this correspondence as a matter of experience simply, rather than of true judgement verified in experience. It was characteristic of early twentieth-century empiricism to speak of bodies and minds, and what we think of in general as constituents of the real world, as 'logical constructions' out of sense-experience.[41] This way of talking brings out very well the respect in which knowledge of what we usually think of as the real world is a matter not just of passive reception of experience, but of intelligent and reasonable mental activity with respect to it. Yet it is liable to be crucially misleading; since it easily leads to the assumption that what we usually think of as the real world does not actually exist prior to the imposition by conscious beings of mental constructions upon their experience, and that all that does really exist in the last analysis is experience itself.[42]

But to infer this directly from the constructive role of the mind in the acquisition of knowledge is to confuse experience with judgement, correspondence$_2$ with correspondence$_1$, and what is merely the necessary *basis* of our *knowledge* of the real world with the real world itself. What is 'given', in the sense of reality or the facts as they are prior to our knowledge, is to be known on the basis of what is 'given' in experience, by attention to the latter, accompanied by intelligent conception and reasonable judgement. It is harmless, and in some circumstances (such as argument with naive realists) instructive, to put it that knowledge of the world is to be had by mental or logical constructions out of sensation, if it is understood (as it is not by idealists or phenomenalists) that it does not follow that what is generally thought of as the real world is itself a mental construction of ours, but rather that it is to be *got at*, to be *progressively known*, through the propounding and testing of such mental constructions.

For the judgement that a certain object is present to have sufficient grounds for being asserted, certain sensations, commonly including sensations *as of* it, must have been enjoyed in the past or be being enjoyed in the present; and for it to be confirmed, certain similar sensations have to be enjoyed in the future. Such are the grounds *in* experience which typically justify the belief that a physical object or state of affairs which *would* exist or obtain *independently* of anyone's experience both exists or obtains and is as it is. But from this it should *not* be inferred that the *meaning of* the statement that some physical object exists or state of affairs obtains is *that* certain experiences have been enjoyed or will be or would in certain circumstances be enjoyed. For p logically to entail q is one thing; for q to be grounds for asserting p is another.

It is one thing to be a potential object of experience; it is another to be a potential object of intelligent conception and reasonable affirmation on the basis of experience; and this is the difference between the mere sum of potential objects of experience on the one hand, and the real world on the other. A priori, the world is, and cannot but be, what conscious subjects or persons tend to come to know by intelligent and reasonable inquiry into their experience. Intelligent inquiry is a matter of the active creation of hypotheses. The presence of such mental constructions in our coming to know, and what is to be made of this, has been something of a crux in the development of philosophy. The naive realist, of course, is not troubled by any problem of knowledge; it never occurs to him to doubt that the real world is what is there to be perceived, which we fail to perceive if we go on with our own ideas rather than looking about us. One may

distinguish three stages in the development of critical awareness
about the nature of knowledge, and consequently about the basic
nature of the world which is nothing other than what is to be
known, each represented by well-known figures in the history of
philosophy.[43] At the first stage, it is apparent that the qualities
which we immediately perceive things as having are rather the
effects of them on our sense-organs, than belonging to the things
themselves; their real nature is to be known through scientific inquiry. At the second stage, it becomes clear that this 'real nature'
of things is just as dependent upon the mental constructions
of scientific theorists as their apparent nature is dependent on
our sense-organs; things in themselves, as they really are independently of human experience and human understanding,
are acknowledged to exist, but claimed to be utterly inscrutable as
to their nature. At the third stage, it is apparent that the postulation of such things-in-themselves makes no sense; while the
sensible world is admittedly mere appearance, the world of the
scientist is nothing but a mental construction. However, it is
possible to move to a fourth stage, of a fully critical account of
knowledge which is at once self-consistent, and able to avoid both
naive realism and the idealism of the third stage. This is a matter
of adverting to and applying the principle which I have tried to
establish − that the real world, the world as it largely is prior to
the gaining of knowledge about it by members of human
societies, is nothing but what progressively comes to be known by
attentiveness to experience, intelligence in hypothesis, and
reasonableness in judgement. While the real is not mere experience, and while mental construction is a necessary element in
human knowledge, at least human mental constructions may be
more or less corroborated as knowledge *in* experience (cor-
respondence$_2$), *of* the world (correspondence$_1$).

The first stage, whose classical expression is the philosophy of
Locke,[44] might be set out as follows: 'When one reflects on the
nature of the real world in relation to our perception of it,
especially with the benefit of scientific knowledge, it becomes
clear that what we directly perceive is not the world as it actually
is, and would have been independently of our perception of it; but
the result of the effect of that world upon our senses. Suppose I
am looking at a cherry tree in spring, hearing the rustle of its
branches in the breeze, and smelling its blossom. It is evident on
reflection that the direct object of my sight is not the tree itself, but

rather the state of affairs brought about in my eye and brain by the impact of the light coming from the tree; and so too with its sound and smell in relation to my ears, my nose, and the related parts of my brain. The tree cannot itself be the direct object of our perceptions, or it would cease to exist when our perceptions of it did so; but it is absurd to deny that the tree exists independently of my senses or anyone else's, and might have thus existed even if we had never been in such a position and circumstances as to have our senses affected by it. We must distinguish, then, between the nature and properties of the tree as it really is in itself; and the nature and properties of the tree as mere appearances to the senses. The former is not directly given to the senses, but is (progressively) known through scientific discovery'.[45]

At the second stage, represented notably by Kant, one argues something like this: 'What has just been said treats scientists as though they had some kind of hot line to reality, to things in themselves. But how could this be the case, given that the scientist has just the same sensory equipment as the ordinary man? He has no sixth sense; and even if he had, it is difficult to see how he could claim for it any privileged position above the other five, to inform him of what really is so as opposed to what merely appears to be so. How, after all, does the scientist proceed? He *constructs* theories, which enable him to *anticipate* future perceptions more accurately than would otherwise be possible, and to *perform* successfully such operations such as building bridges, manufacturing explosives, and sending men to the moon. Thus scientific theories are essentially mental constructions which we may put to effective practical use in anticipating experience and manipulating the world for our convenience; it is sheer superstition to suppose that it puts us directly in touch with a real world as opposed to the merely apparent world of everyday experience.[46] Certainly there *is* a world of real things, prior to and independent of our experience and of the mental constructions which we impose upon it; but it is and must remain utterly unknown to us.'

The epistemologist at the third stage will say: 'I agree with all of what has just been said apart from the last sentence. What is really implied by the course of the argument is that the notion that there are any things in themselves, with no relation to our sensations and the mental constructions which we base upon them, is incoherent. In the last analysis the world is a construction of thought rather than something which can be distinguished from and then compared with thought, in such a way that a judgement might be true so far as it "corresponds" with it, false so far as it fails to do so. Truth is a matter of coherence within a system of judgements, and not of correspondence with a reality supposed to exist independently of thought or language'.[47]

It will be useful to set out these stages in terms of the mental capacities which I mentioned above as essential for the acquisition of knowledge. One may put it that the naive realist and the phenomenalist exaggerate the role of attentiveness in our getting to know the world; the naive realist assuming that the real world is directly apprehended by means of it, the phenomenalist, more justly, that it provides us merely with a raw material of sensation upon which our 'logical constructions' are to be imposed. The idealist exaggerates the role of intelligence; he sees like the phenomenalist that mental constructions are involved in getting to know what is usually conceived of as the independent and external world, and infers from this that the latter is not really 'independent' or 'external' at all. But if the naive realist neglects the role of intelligence in getting to know, the idealist neglects that of reason. Not only do we have intelligently to frame hypotheses about the world if we are to get to know it; we must reasonably determine which of the hypotheses we have framed is the most likely to be true of the world as it really is. The evidence on this is apt to be provided by experience. But this does *not* entail that the real world is after all, in spite of the criticism brought forward by the idealist, simply the object of experience, whether actual or potential. It is what *is to be intelligently conceived and reasonably affirmed on the basis of experience.*

Those at the first stage rightly advert to the fact that the world which we claim to know is by no means identical with the world that we perceive; and contrast the latter as appearance with the former as reality. Those at the second stage rightly point out that what we claim to know over and above what we perceive involves mental construction on our part; and thus admitting that the world as directly perceived is mere appearance, and that the world as we claim to know it is a mental construction based on appearance, despair of attaining knowledge of things as they really are. At the third stage, one infers from this that such 'things as they really are' apart from any relation to experience and mental construction are sheer illusion. But according to the fully critical account of knowledge, 'things as they really are' are nothing more or less than what conscious subjects tend progressively to come to know by propounding and testing mental constructions on the basis of and in relation to experience. With the naive realist and those at the first stage, against those at the second and third stages, the exponent of the fully critical account of knowledge believes that there is a real world independent of and prior to the sensations and mental constructions of conscious human subjects. With those at the first stage, he agrees that one tends to get to know the nature of this world through scientific method (which is nothing other than a sustained and stringent application of intelligence and reasonableness to experience) issuing in scientific theory. With those at the second and third stages, he admits the element of mental construction, and the consequent *a priori* assumptions (the world must be such we *can* get to know it by means of such mental constructions arising from and tested in relation to experience, with all that *that* entails) involved in our getting to know the world.

These aspects of the problem of knowledge which have long bedevilled philosophy have their exact counterparts in the writings of contemporary sociologists. It is obvious enough, when one reflects on the matter, that the scheme of concepts through which anyone apprehends the world depends very largely at least on the society within which he lives.[48] It is clear also that radically different conceptual schemes are found to be prevalent in different societies. One may choose to emphasise the fact of the 'social construction' of the everyday world, and contrast it with the 'real world' discovered by scientists; but it does not take much further reflection to make it apparent that the conceptual schemes of scientists are just as liable to social determination as those of ordinary people. Some sociologists have admitted that the 'worlds' taken for granted by men of common sense and postulated by scientists are both socially determined; but have insisted all the same, in a manner analogous to that of Kant, that there is actually a real world quite independent of society.[49] But it is difficult to see why this insistence, and the very conception of such a 'real world' supposed to exist quite independent of social factors, from which the socially determined 'worlds' of common sense and of science are supposed to be quite distinct, should not be just as socially determined as are these latter 'worlds'.[50] However, if the basic problem is the same in sociology as in philosophy, so is its solution. The real world, as it existed and exists largely prior to and independently of human societies, is nothing other than what members of these societies tend to come to know so far as the dispositions of attentiveness, intelligence and reasonableness are assiduously cultivated in those societies. (At this rate a mentally indolent man in a highly civilised society would be liable to know much more than a savage who was a prodigy of intellectual virtue.) To explain the set of beliefs characteristic of a society is to show how far they are to be accounted for as due to attentiveness, intelligence and reasonableness, and how far as due to interference in the exercise of these capacities by other factors such as fear, tradition, deference to authority or class ideology.[51]

At the second and third stages, it becomes very clear that the world as we come to know it, notably by scientific method, is a mental construction. But common sense, along with naive realism and those at the first stage, would agree with a more thorough analysis in protesting that at least it is not *our* mental construction; since *our* mental constructions have to be tested for correspondence$_1$ with it, through correspondence$_2$ with our experience, as more or less true or false. And the evidence that the world *is* a mental construction, but not *our* mental construction, forms the basis, as I shall argue, of a cosmological argument for theism.

M. K. Munitz has argued that we can have no good reason to suppose that the universe as conceived in terms of any cosmological theory corresponds to, or even approximates to, the real universe. He distinguishes between the 'universe$_1$', as the real universe, of which the observed universe forms a part, from the 'universe$_2$', as what may be postulated in any cosmological model constructed by the human intellect; such a distinction, he says, enables one to avoid begging the question of whether cosmological models should be interpreted in a realistic way. After all, the cosmologist cannot inspect the universe, as he might a particular object within it, to see whether his model represents it or how accurately it does so; at best, his model may yield some predictions which are confirmed, or be of greater aesthetic appeal than some rival model. He concludes that whether the universe is literally an intelligibly structured whole is a question incapable of resolution. Of course, it is easy to see why people are prone to accept the view that the 'universe$_1$' actually *is* an intelligible structure. 'Man reads into the world as already there, a completely unified structure that would fill out those partial successes, and incomplete fragments of intelligibility, he has already managed to establish in patches of his experience. Analogy, vision, and faith come to support the projection of what is a human need into an allegedly antecedent ontologic fact.'[52]

In spite of Kant's demonstration that the conception of the universe as an intelligible structure is to be accepted only as a regulative ideal for the scientist, Munitz complains that the belief that it, what he calls the universe$_1$, really *is* such, has been influential right up to our own time. Einstein's lifelong search for a unified field theory, and the view which he expressed that the universe is a 'puzzle to be solved', are striking illustrations of the point. Munitz concedes that it would be just as unwarranted dogmatically to *deny* that the actual universe is characterised by such a comprehensive order as to *assert* it. The universe$_1$ *may* be of such a nature. All that can properly be claimed is that we do not have, and cannot ever hope to have, any evidence that it *is* so. It is possible that the world contains elements of disorder which would for ever frustrate the human longing for total understanding. One may properly maintain that the observed world is intelligible so far as science has actually reduced it to intelligibility. But this implies nothing about the wider world of which the world observed by us forms a part.[53]

It might be insisted all the same that science presupposes and confirms the assumptions that the 'universe$_1$' really is intelligible as a whole. Now recent developments in the philosophy of science, deriving from the work of Poincaré, Duhem and others, have emphasised the importance of theories in science, as opposed to mere reports of observations and experiments. Munitz infers from these developments that scientific theories are 'free intellectual creative constructions', which 'feed upon models and analogies of various sorts, and are to be judged not in terms of any test of literal correspondence with the facts, but in terms of their general utility and pragmatic fruitfulness'. They are not to be proven true or false; nor does it make sense to speak of 'their being successive approximations to some inherent structure of reality'. What applies to the scientist applies *a fortiori* to the metaphysician; if the former cannot compare his speculations with the contents of the world, to see whether they get them right or wrong, no more can the latter. 'Like scientific theories, metaphysical theories cannot be shown to be wrong, in the sense of literally falsified. They can only be shown to be less consistent, less useful, less rich in conceptual connections, less comprehensive in their range, or founded on key analogies that are less deployable and fertile than those contained in other metaphysical theories.' Metaphysicians are to be assessed like artists, for the beauty, audacity and range of their mental constructions; to regard them as in the business of propounding the truth about things is to be involved in insuperable difficulties.[54]

Against Munitz's contrast between the 'universe$_1$' and any 'universe$_2$', or even what might be approximated to to a greater or lesser degree by such a 'universe$_2$', the main objection to be made is the same as that made by Hegel against the Kantian 'thing-in-itself';[55] the conception of a 'real universe', of what Munitz calls a 'universe$_1$', is no less a conceptual construction than that of any 'universe$_2$'. But what kind of conception is that of the real or actual universe? As I have been arguing, it can in the last resort be nothing other than that of what tends to come to be known, so far as the mental processes by which we come to know, and to which the achievements of the sciences are due, are followed through indefinitely. What seems to underlie Munitz's account is a view, such as I have argued to be incoherent on the last analysis,[56] of the real universe as somehow *other than* what is thus to be known. It is true that we cannot, as it might be expressed, get a clear first-order conception of the universe as a whole, simply because we do not know all of it. But it does not follow from this that we cannot obtain a clear second-order conception of it, as that which we tend to get to know so far as we follow the appropriate methods and procedures. Munitz's thoroughgoing agnosticism about the nature of the world as it really is seems based on his failure to grasp this fundamental point.

Munitz's claim that scientific theories are to be evaluated not as representing the truth about things, or even as approximating to such a representation, but rather for such virtues as elegance, usefulness and the capacity to predict phenomena, seems to be based upon a false antithesis. It also appears to result from oversight of the distinction pointed out earlier[57] between correspondence$_1$, which obtains between a true statement and the fact by virtue of which it is true, and correspondence$_2$, which obtains between evidence and a statement corroborated by that evidence. When a court of law is trying to establish whether a defendant is guilty of murder, the committing of the murder by the defendant (which, if it happened at all, is an event of the past) is one thing, the evidence available to the court which bears on the matter (which consists of what is observable in the present) another. But no reputable judge, jury or detective would regard the elegance, usefulness or economy of the verdict in accounting for the evidence as in the least significant, *except* as rendering it more or less likely that the defendant actually did or did not commit the crime with which he has been charged. Similarly, a serious palæontologist is concerned with elegant and economical ways of accounting for presently-available evidence deemed relevant to his specialty, only as a means of finding out how it is likely to have been with therapsid reptiles, ichthyosauri or whatever. But if it would be misguided in these last kinds of case, to drive a wedge between predicting and explaining data in an acceptable manner on the one hand, and coming to state the truth on the other, it is difficult to see why it should be any less so in the case of scientific theory.

If the theoretical scientist, in spite of Munitz's contentions, need not despair of coming to speak the truth about things, or at least of coming closer to doing so, the main basis for Munitz's view, that the metaphysician is not really in the business of making truth-claims, collapses. The metaphysician may gain some conception of the basic nature and structure of the real world, not indeed by taking a look at it as he might at black-necked grebes or the Taj Mahal, but by extrapolation from what are and cannot but be, on the pain of the self-destructiveness of judgement itself, the right procedures for coming to know. He can then contrast with this empiricist and idealist accounts, each of which emphasise some elements in the process of coming to know at the expense of others.[58] Munitz's own account seems a curious mixture of idealism, naive realism, and a Kant-like doctrine of the world, or perhaps an aspect of the world, as ultimately eluding in principle all our attempts to come to know it. Thus according to him the world as conceived by metaphysicians and theoretical scientists is a more or less aesthetically appealing or practically useful mental construction; only the observable objects of naive realism, and the mysterious world-in-itself (Munitz's 'universe$_1$'), seem to enjoy existence prior to and independently of actual or potential human thought.[59]

There is an interesting question about the status of Munitz's conclusions, on his own account. Can *they* aspire to truth? He argues for them skilfully and at length, adducing evidence, pointing out different ways in which it might be accounted for, and commending his own views as the most satisfactory available account. But this seems to presuppose assumptions about the nature of truth, and therefore about the world which is what is to be known through the medium of true judgement, that are similar to those for which I have been arguing, and incompatible with those of Munitz himself.

It will be objected that what I have been saying leaves materialism out of account. But it seems to me that 'materialism' is a word of many meanings, which are apt to be confused with one another in metaphysical arguments. 'Matter' as that which all real beings are supposed to consist of or depend on tends to play the role of *ens a se*, first cause or unproduced producer in many metaphysical schemes and world-views.[60] The term is used in at least the following distinct senses:

(1) the 'stuff' out of which things are made;
(2) the basic particles of which things consist;
(3) the direct object of sense experience;[61]
(4) what physics and chemistry are about;
(5) what exists prior to and independently of the human mind; and
(6) what exists prior to and independently of any mind whatever.[62]

Matter as stuff is whatever things are made out of. The 'stuff' out of which some things are made seems in turn to be made out of other kinds of stuff; thus human bodies are made out of animal tissue, animal tissue out of organic compounds, organic compounds out of chemical elements, and chemical elements out of fundamental particles. It is notable that there is a department of science concerned with each of these types of 'matter', which brings out the connection between senses (1) and (4); it seems right to say that physics and chemistry are studies of the nature of the 'stuff' out of which things are made. The relation of 'matter' in sense (3) to 'matter' in senses (1) and (4) does seem to give rise to serious confusion; gold and carbon as known to the ordinary man are in one sense the same, in another sense by no means the same, as these substances as conceived by the chemist; along the lines of what has already been argued, it may be said that 'matter' as perceived by the ordinary man (sense (3)) gives rise to questions, and its properties are ultimately to be explained, through the operation of intelligence and reason, as 'matter' as conceived by the scientist (sense (4)). While the latter is of a number of types, which constitute a hierarchy of which the higher depend for existence on the lower, only that which is at the lowest level — and hence is the 'stuff' of which every material thing and every other kind of 'stuff' may be said to consist — is 'matter' in sense (2).

The difference between senses (5) and (6) is of considerable importance for our present purposes. It is one thing to insist, in opposition to idealism, that material things in general exist and are what they are prior to and independently of the human mind; it is quite another to claim, in contradiction to theism (or polytheism or polydaemonism) that material things in general do or can exist prior to and independently of mind of any kind. That is to say, from the falsity of idealism, which entails the non-existence of matter in sense (5), the falsity of theism, which entails its non-existence in sense (6), by no means immediately follows. On the contrary, it is a consequence of theism, and of the doctrine of creation which is an aspect of it, that 'matter' in sense (5) does exist.[63] Another significant fact about 'matter' is to be noted in the light of our previous discussion. Although Berkeley seems to have been wrong in holding that 'to be is to be perceived or to perceive', he did draw attention in a striking way to the manner in which whatever is real must have at least a potential relation to the thought of conscious subjects or persons.[64] Whatever 'matter' is, so far as it is real at all, it must be some part or aspect of what is to be conceived and affirmed by conscious subjects on the basis of their experience.

At least equally relevant to the cosmological argument as the concept of 'matter' is that of 'cause'. There have been many accounts of causation in the history of philosophy, and this is not the place to attempt a survey of them. But it is worth noting that accounts of causation tend to lie between two extremes, one forcefully and notoriously presented in the work of Hume, the other due above all to Aristotle.[65] According to Hume, all human knowledge is based upon 'impressions', by which he means either data of sensation such as those directly present to sight, hearing, touching and so on, or states of consciousness such as delight, fear and the feeling of anger. All the 'ideas' of which our knowledge consists are faint copies of past 'impressions', by means of which we may remember or anticipate 'impressions' of the past or the future. Our more complex 'ideas' are built up out of simple 'ideas', each of which must be a copy of some 'impression' which we have enjoyed in the past. Thus I can have an 'idea' of, and perhaps even expect to see on your garden wall, a blue tomato, if I have at some time enjoyed an 'impression' of blue, and 'impressions' of all the visual and tactile qualities which go to make up a tomato. This example illustrates how, on Hume's account, I may have a conception of or belief about an object of which I have had no experience, provided only that I have enjoyed 'impressions' corresponding to each of the simple 'ideas' from which my comlex 'idea' of that object is built up.[66]

Hume goes on to argue that we have no 'impression' of the relation between causes and their effects, and consequently no 'idea' of it. When we consider the case of a moving billiard ball which hits one that is stationary, causing the latter to move; or of a brick striking a window, with the consequence that the window is shattered; we may at first suppose that we can actually perceive the causal relation between the one event and the other. But a little reflection will show that this is not the case. What actually happens is this. We have very often seen one ball in motion hitting another that is stationary, and the second then moving; or at least successions of events closely analogous to this. The same applies *mutatis mutandis* in the case of the brick and the pane of glass. So, when we perceive an event of the former kind in each case, we are strongly inclined by habit to expect an event of the latter kind, which indeed does occur. Where we go wrong is in supposing that we perceive some actual *connection* between the two events, as opposed to their mere *concomitance*; the only connection is in the habit of our mind by which we expect an event of the second kind to follow an event of the first kind.[67]

One might be inclined to accept an account like Hume's of the causal relation between events which are external to ourselves; but to protest that there is one kind of case at least in which we have direct experience of the link between causes and their effects. When I decide to open my mouth, and duly it opens, or I decide to raise my arm, and it goes up accordingly, it is surely the case, it may be argued, that I have a direct apprehension not only of my act of will and my overt action, but of the connection between them. This was maintained by Berkeley, who inferred that the only justifiable conception of causality we have is that of the will of a spirit, that is to say, of some kind of conscious agent. He concluded that all events which were not due to the agency of visible conscious subjects such as men and women must be due to invisible conscious subjects such as God or angels.[68] However, Hume denied that we have any more experience of a causal connection between volition and action than of any other kind of causal connection. No doubt it has always, or at least very usually, been the case, that the raising of my arm has followed directly upon my decision then to raise my arm, except where there has been some assignable impediment to its being raised; and this has given rise in me to the confident expectation that the same pattern of events will always occur in future. But there is nothing incoherent about the expectation that, in future, the will to raise my arm will always be followed promptly, for example, by the raising of my foot, or even by an alteration in the positions of the sun or the stars. That the will to raise my arm has always been followed by the raising of my arm, except where there has been some assignable hindrance, in the past, provides no rationally compelling proof that it will do so in the future. Once again, it becomes apparent on reflection that the causal connection under discussion is reducible to a habit of mind based upon the experience of a constant conjunction between types of event.[69]

On Hume's account of causation, there is no difficulty whatever in showing that argument from the world of our experience as a whole as effect to God as cause must be fallacious. For the essence of causal reasoning is that one has often perceived (an event of type) A to be followed by (an event of type) B; and never A not followed by B, or B not preceded by A; so, the next time we perceive B, we maintain that A has preceded it; or the next time we perceive A, that B will follow it. Thus, for us to have any basis for arguing that the event of the coming into existence of a world must have been due to the creative act of a God, we would have to have witnessed a number of creative acts by God or gods, with worlds coming into existence immediately afterwards. But God's creation of the world is supposed to be unique, so there could not have been any such a collection of successions of events; and even if there had been, in the nature of the case, no creature could have witnessed an event of such a kind.[70]

It might be objected to this that, though to be sure we have no experiences or 'impressions' of divine creativity — we have never seen, heard or smelt gods creating worlds — we do have experience of something analogous, in human agency. Causal reasoning, if it is to be of much use to us, cannot demand that, in the case where we state with adequate reason that there is a causal relation between event of type A and event of type B, the case of A and the case of B must be *in all respects whatever* like the previous cases of which we have had experience. It is most improbable that such a demand could ever be met, since no billiard ball is exactly like any other billiard ball. Given that exact similarity between relevant cases is not to be demanded for causal reasoning to be applicable, one might plead that the analogy between the universe as a whole and a human artefact is sufficiently close for us to be able to argue that, as we have always found by experience that things like the latter are due to intelligent design, the same must apply to the former; and the intelligent designer of the universe is what people mean by God.

However, the colossal disproportion between the alleged divine 'artefact' which is the universe, and human artefacts which form such a tiny and insignificant part of it, makes the comparison on which the argument turns questionable indeed. Where one is trying to argue from the existence of an effect of type B^1 to the operation of a cause of type A^1, on the basis of previous experience of the causation of events of type B by causes of type A, it seems obvious enough that the greater the difference between B and B^1, the less justifiable the inference. And even granted that there is a case for maintaining that the world as a whole is any more like one aspect of the tiny part of it with which we are acquainted than like another, it is by no means obvious that human artefacts are in a position of privilege in this respect. We find some adjustment of means to ends in the universe at large, as we do in human artefacts; but we also find such adjustment in living organisms. Is not the universe as a whole, so far as we are justified in making such comparisons at all, at least as analogous to an animal or to a vegetable as to a human artefact? If this is so, one might as justifiably say that the world owes its origin to something like procreation or seeding, as with the animals and vegetables of our experience, as that it does so to something like intelligent design. That all such accounts are as plausible and as vulnerable as one another tends to show that all reasonings supposed to establish the nature of the cause or causes of the universe as a whole, or even whether such a cause or such causes exist, must be fruitless.[71]

That the Humean analysis of causation is destructive of causal arguments for the existence of God is thus clear enough; but it has to be remarked that the difficulties to which it gives rise are by no means confined to natural theology. If a physicist sees a streak on a photographic plate, he may properly say that it was caused by the passage of a fundamental particle. But no one has ever seen or heard a proton or an electron, let alone seen the passing of one followed by the occurrence of a streak. Again, if I perceive one of my colleagues making noises or gestures or marks on paper, I may properly explain these as due to, or caused by, his thoughts, feelings, decisions and so on. But I have never seen or felt, or had any other kind of direct experience of, another person's thoughts, feelings or decisions. But on Hume's analysis, to argue from effects to causes one has to have had experiences, or 'impressions', of previous examples of the cause as well as of the effect. It seems, then, that both scientists in the course of their professional work, and ordinary people in the natural course of life, talk and argue in a manner in which, if Hume's analysis of causation were correct, they would not be able to do. One might say that the most important upshot of Hume's work is the *reductio ad absurdum* of the assumption that our knowledge can go no further than our experience, and that this is brought out with special vividness in his treatment of causality. However, much of his work amounts to an attempt to mask these consequences of the basic principles of his thought;[72] a trend followed by many of his admirers.[73]

I have already argued at length that things and events of the past, the thoughts and feelings of other persons, and fundamental particles, have in common that, while they are not themselves perceivable, they are to be intelligently conceived and reasonably affirmed as *explaining why* perceivable things and events are as they are, as providing *sufficient reason why* they are so. This brings us straight to the second of the two basic conceptions of the nature of causation mentioned above, that due to Aristotle. The 'cause' of anything, according to Aristotle, is the correct answer to the question *why* it exists or is as it is. Aristotle in fact extends this analysis even to questions like 'What is an X?', which he treats as reducible to the question 'Why is *this* an X?', where 'this' refers to any individual thing which we may encounter. For example, at this rate the questions 'What is a man?' and 'What is a house?' may be tackled by asking 'Why is this aggregate of flesh, blood, bones and so on a man?' and 'Why is this collection of building materials a house?' The correct answer to this kind of question 'why?', why it is that any object is of the particular kind that it is, is what Aristotle called the 'formal cause'.[74] Other types of question 'Why?', which are more directly relevant to our usual modern conceptions of cause, are concerned with the reason why something exists or some state of affairs obtains. For example, in the case of a house, one would have to ask, in order to give a reasonably full account of why it existed and was as it was, who constructed it, to what design, out of what material, and for what purpose. The correct answers to these questions would be what Aristotle would term respectively the efficient cause, the exemplary cause, the material cause, and the final cause. We gain knowledge of such causes, according to Aristotle, by asking with respect to the things of our experience the two sorts of question already described.[75]

It will be obvious, from what has been said, that Aristotle's conception of causes and of our knowledge of them is consistent with the account of knowledge in general which we have given, whereas Hume's is not. And it does not appear that Aristotle's conception gives rise to the paradoxes that Hume's notoriously does. It remains to be seen whether an account such as Aristotle's provides any basis for claiming that the world as a whole has a cause, and that this cause is God.

The most celebrated compromise between these extreme positions on the nature of causality is that of Kant. His conception seems to amount to the following. All sensible events *must* in some sense have causes. How are we to understand this 'must'? The proposition that all events have causes does not seem to be analytic, as the proposition that all *effects* have causes may reasonably be supposed to be so. Hume has shown clearly enough that we have no *experience of* the causal relation itself; yet it seems an inadequate account of the matter, and indeed one ultimately destructive of most of our claims to knowledge, to conclude, as Hume did, that the causal relation has no firmer foundation than our acquired mental habit of associating the occurrence of one kind of observed event with that of another. Kant concludes that the necessity of the causal relation derives from the fact that, by the very nature of our cognitive faculties, we cannot but think of the world of our experience in terms of it. The consequence of this is that the causal relation has no bearing on things in themselves, as they might be apart from their mediation through our sensation and the forms of our understanding. This makes it inadmissible to apply the principle 'Every event has a cause', so necessary to the prosecution of empirical science, otherwise than within the world of experience; for example, as premiss of a proof that human freedom is impossible, since human actions, being caused in common with all other events of experience, cannot be other than as they are; or that there must be a Cause of the world of experience as a whole.[76]

From the point of view of the argument of this chapter, of course, it is to be retorted that, since the Humean problem about our knowledge of causation is based upon a misapprehension, there need be no Kantian solution to that problem; we get to know the nature and the properties of the real world which is independent of our experience, including the causal relations between the things and events constitutive of it, by inquiry into the things and events of our experience. If the question of what causes the existence of the world as a whole is an illegitimate question, it will not be for reasons which presuppose a denial of this truth.

It might be objected that we have still not established that knowledge is actually possible at all; that we have provided no argument against the thoroughgoing sceptic, who denies its possibility.[77] The tactic proposed by Aristotle for dealing with sceptics still seems the best available;[78] that is, to get them to talk. Suppose that the sceptic is induced to say something, for example that scepticism is true, or that knowledge is impossible. He may then be asked whether he (or his authority) has attended to the evidence on the matter; whether he has exerted his intelligence in thinking up ways in which that evidence might be accounted for; and whether he has reasonably judged that his conclusion that scepticism is true, or that knowledge is impossible, is the way that best accounts for it. If he has done all of these things, and justifies his conclusions on this basis, he is implicitly committed to the view that one tends to get to know what is so by intelligent and reasonable assessment of evidence – a principle subversive of scepticism. If he has not, there is no reason to take his scepticism seriously. If he only implies that at least most of what is called knowledge falls short of absolute certainty, and is to that extent subject to doubt;[79] and that we ought constantly to be alive to the possibility of error if we are to come to know what is true; then what he is saying is probably true and important. But such a view by no means entails the impossibility of knowledge except on an implausibly narrow definition of 'knowledge'. 'People' will turn out not to be not quite so abundant as is generally supposed, if you insist that all *real* people have red hair.

Perhaps the proponent of scepticism will protest that he only means to be sceptical about claims as to how the world *really* is, how things are *in themselves*; as opposed to how the world *seems* to *us*, or what it is practical for us to believe about things. But, as I have already argued,[80] the meaningfulness of such a distinction presupposes that at least in principle we do have means of getting at the real truth about the world, or about things as they really are, which may be more or less thoroughly applied. As a result of applying them more thoroughly than another person, or of attending to others who have done so, I may often have reason to assert that what I believe is probably the truth about how things are, as far as it goes, whereas what he believes is merely apparently so, or no more than a convenient fiction. Indeed I may and do have excellent grounds for holding that many of the beliefs which I hold now will at some time in future be relegated to this status by a more thorough application of these principles than I have myself achieved, or has been achieved by anyone in my community.

At the opposite extreme from scepticism is the view that knowledge can be taken for granted, and needs no justification. Why should one search for the foundations of knowledge, it may be asked, or assume that knowledge needs such foundations?[81] Is not the hankering after such 'foundations' a mere relic of a superstitious (albeit rather recent) philosophical past, when knowledge of physical objects was supposed to be 'founded' on 'sense-data' or something of the kind — for all that the nature of these alleged foundations, and how they could be foundations for knowledge, were never satisfactorily determined? It may be concluded from these reflections that knowledge has no foundations, and that to seek them is consequently to pursue a chimera.

But one who denies that knowledge has or needs foundations may yet concede that not all cases of what people count as 'knowledge' are really such. It would seem at least as paradoxical to hold that everything which was ever counted as knowledge really was knowledge, as to hold that everything which was ever identified as gold really was gold. The fact is that some people have confidently maintained to be knowledge what other people have strenuously denied to be such. Assuming that in such cases both parties cannot be right, the question arises of which of them is wrong, and why; and so, more generally, by virtue of what features some claimants to the title of knowledge really deserve it, others not. This would presumably be settled either by appeal to social convention, with consequences already discussed;[82] or by reference partly to the truth of the beliefs concerned, partly to the method by which those beliefs were arrived at. But to spell out basic methods by which one arrives at those beliefs which are to be counted as knowledge is nothing else than to assign foundations to knowledge in the relevant sense.

Those who impugn the assumption that knowledge has or needs foundations are often attacking the view that it is 'sense-data' or some close equivalent which provide such foundations; but it is one thing to believe that knowledge has foundations, another to believe that these foundations consist partly or wholly of 'sense-data' or any close equivalent. It will be noticed that in presenting a sketch of what the foundations of knowledge are, I did not refer to the 'sense-data' which were so conspicuous a feature of those foundations as conceived a few decades ago. I am concerned to provide an account of knowledge which stresses both how far what we know goes beyond what we perceive or could possibly perceive, and the means by which our knowledge is able to go beyond our perception, however narrowly or broadly perception and its objects may be conceived. I did not wish to get entangled in the notorious philosophical thicket of the problem of 'sense-data', when it seemed possible to say enough for present purposes about knowledge, its nature and justification, without becoming so. The reason why it is unnecessary to postulate 'sense-data', in setting out and justifying the account of knowledge given here, is that physical objects and states of affairs as perceived could be the 'data' to which questions are addressed, and in relation to which possible answers may be tested, which issue in that knowledge which goes beyond perception and its objects in the manner already described. Yet it does seem worthwhile, in order to clarify and set in a broader context what has already been said, to relate the present account of knowledge and its foundations to that which does postulate the occurrence of sense-data.

Let us say that one 'perceives' X when all of the following conditions are fulfilled: when one has a sensation as of X, when X is
actually present where one supposes it to be, and where X causes
the sensation as of X.[83] One is tempted to say that sensation as of
X is grounds for the judgement, or provides foundations for the
judgement, that X is present where one supposes it to be.[84]
However, it is rightly argued that unless our language were
primarily about perceivable objects in a shared public world, we
would not be able to talk about our sensations *as* of such objects;
we could not find out about sense-data first, and then about
physical objects on the basis of this, so in this sense sense-data
cannot provide foundations for our more ordinary forms of
knowledge. Further, it is suggested that if sensation is taken to
provide grounds for our knowledge of physical objects, an infinite
regress is more or less inevitable.[85] If our sensations are
themselves objects of knowledge, and knowledge must have
grounds, then the knowledge of our sensations must have
grounds; and the knowledge of *those* grounds must have grounds;
and so on *ad infinitum*. On the other hand, if we do not have
knowledge of our sensations, then this cannot provide an adequate basis for the rest of our knowledge. To avoid this dilemma,
the claim may be made that there is one kind of knowledge
which does not require grounds, the direct kind of knowledge
('knowledge by acquaintance' as Russell called it[86]) which we
have of our sensations; and an indirect kind of knowledge which
we may have on the basis of this, which does require grounds. To
this claim it may be retorted that it is an abuse of words to claim
that one knows *directly* the kind of thing which in normal circumstances one would not be said to know at all — that one is
having a dull ache in one's calf, or a bright magenta spot in
the centre of one's visual field — and that one knows only in-
directly the kind of thing which would normally count as
'knowledge' — like the age of one's children and the location of
one's place of work. Thus Wittgenstein maintained, in *On Certainty*, that one can only *know* that some state of affairs is the case
when it makes sense to doubt it.[87] Evidently his view consorts
rather well with the account of knowledge which we have been
advancing; where knowledge is a case of reasonable selection
among possibilities, and doubt presumably a matter of some
hesitation between them.

I think that the solution to the puzzle about the grounds of knowledge is that while knowledge of its nature does require grounds, the grounds of knowledge need not themselves in all cases be objects of knowledge. What one *perceives*, in the sense given in the last paragraph, one also knows to be the case or to exist; since perception of an object (and so *mutatis mutandis* for a state of affairs) implies that the judgement that the object is present is true, and that the perceiver has grounds for the judgement in his sensations as of the object.[88] Other possible explanations, analogous to those which explain why the patient suffering from *delirium tremens* has sensations as of pink rats, have, *ex hypothesi*, less to commend them. But one does not characteristically know the content of one's sensations as such; to come to a judgement about these, as opposed to a judgement about the physical objects and states of affairs for knowledge of which they provide grounds, one needs a special kind of attention. Pain is a special case; judgement that one is in pain (*pace* Wittgenstein[89]) is really quite common, because one's subjective state, as opposed to the state of the physical environment for which one's subjective states provide the evidence, is then forced on one's attention. Where other sorts of sensation are concerned, the case is different; yet I can judge, if I attend to the matter carefully, that I have at present such-and-such visual experiences, or such-and-such tactile sensations in, say, my right foot or left thigh; but I do not generally trouble to do so. Nor *could* I do so, unless there were a public world which provided the primary reference for judgements, and in relation to which the terms which I might use to make this special kind of judgement acquired their meaning in the first instance. We could not talk about pain unless there were publicly-observable behaviour characteristically displayed by those in pain; unless there were real pink objects, the patient would not be able to speak of his sensations as of pink rats to anyone else. I conclude that sensations or 'sense-data' do in one sense provide foundations for knowledge; but it should not be inferred from this that they are what we primarily or in the first instance know, let alone that they are all that we really know.

It has been suggested that Wittgenstein was mistaken in maintaining that we could not know our present states of sensation and feeling; but that all the same he was making an important point in so doing.[90] This would be exactly the conclusion to be drawn from what I have just argued. We *can* know them, though we do not *usually* do so; what we usually know in the first instance are the states of affairs for whose existence or occurrence they provide grounds. If sensations are in some sense direct objects of experience, at least material objects and states of affairs in the public world are the primary objects of *judgements grounded in* experience. However, it must be remembered that the whole of this discussion of the vexed question of sense-data is by way of parenthesis; whichever side one takes on the issue of their occurrence or their importance for the theory of knowledge, the basic argument of this book is not affected. What *is* essential to that argument is that what we know goes beyond what we do or possibly could perceive; whether the *data for* these less immediate forms of knowledge are conceived in terms of raw sensation or perceived physical objects and states of affairs.

What in general are the implications of the 'background conviction', apparently essential to all knowledge whatever, 'that the form of one's discourse reveals something of the structure of the world'?[91] How does this state of affairs come about? Does the form of the world really depend upon the form of our discourse about it? This view is more or less that of Kant (granted that he would, perhaps less misleadingly,[92] have described the matter in terms of thought rather than of language), and has been attributed to the later Wittgenstein.[93] If the form of the world as such is really dependent upon the form of our discourse, it seems to follow that there can be no world of such a form prior to and independent of our discourse. It may be protested, in the manner of Kant on things in themselves, that a world might so exist all the same, but be utterly different from anything that our discourse could possibly be about. But, if this point is properly taken, even *such* a reference to a world which *ex hypothesi* we cannot conceivably refer to must be ruled out. So, apparently, if the basic premiss is accepted that the form of the world is dependent upon the form of our discourse, it seems to follow that our thought and our language must create the world, and that there can be no world independent of our thought and speech about it. Thus it seems to follow that, short of the intolerable paradox just stated, the world must have had the very general overall nature which *enables* us to think and talk about it *prior to* our thinking and talking about it. Does the form of the world, then, somehow directly influence, through our experience, the form taken by our discourse about it? But the arguments of Hume and Kant really do seem to have shown that, short of certain *a priori* assumptions, we cannot know a world; thus we cannot apparently find out what pertains to the basic form of the world, for example that it has a causal structure, *a posteriori*, by experience. It seems to follow that the form must belong *both* to our mental processes as such, *and* to the world as it existed prior to the imposition upon it of our mental processes. There is a mutual fit; and one might put it that what Wittgenstein called 'grammar' must be a sign of metaphysical fact, rather than alleged metaphysical fact being merely the shadow of grammar.[94]

It may be objected that the course of reasoning which I have followed in this chapter violates what Jacques Monod calls 'the principle of objectivity', which is to the effect that logic and experience alone are the sources of genuine knowledge of the world.[95] But the trouble with this principle is its ambiguity. What is to be understood, first, by 'experience'? Is it merely sense-experience? Does it include our moods and feelings? Does it further include the awareness of being puzzled, asking questions, coming to understand, and making judgements and decisions, which are of the essence of our consciousness as intellectual and rational subjects? I shall argue that it is largely due to this last aspect of our 'experience', if it is so to be called, that we have some positive conception of the nature of God. Still more ambiguous is the notion of 'logic'. In a narrow sense, as notoriously was shown by Hume, 'logic' will not take us a step beyond our experience. Mere deduction from states of affairs which can, even on the most generous interpretation of the terms, be said to be objects of our 'experience', will get us nowhere near the propositions confidently, and in my opinion very reasonably, affirmed by men of science. In a wide sense, one may mean by 'logic' the whole apparatus of framing hypotheses, and testing judgements, which is essential over and above attention to experience for the practice of science. But it is precisely what is presupposed in the practice of 'logic' in this wider sense that I have been at pains to bring out in this chapter; 'logic' in a narrow sense, the making of valid deductions, is an essential part of this, but cannot be the whole. 'Logic and experience' in a narrow sense, then, are insufficient for science; 'logic and experience' in the wider sense, I shall try to show, are sufficient to provide a rational basis for theism. If 'experience' in a wide sense gives us a basis for conceiving the nature of God, 'logic' in a wide sense gives us grounds for asserting his existence.

It may be complained in addition that I have misled the reader by talking of such 'inner' and 'private' acts and dispositions as those of attending to sensations, coming to understand, making the testing judgements, and so on; that the upshot of the argument would have been very different had I attended to the 'public' phenomenon of language. The answer to this is, first, that the acts and dispositions which I have claimed to be involved in the acquisition of knowledge are at best equivocally 'private'. Everyone who is conscious is aware of their occurrence; everyone has excellent grounds for attributing them to other people. Further, they are means by which the 'public' world can be investigated and known. Second, the appeal to 'language' is fatally ambiguous. One may mean by the term either merely a string of patterned noises or marks (according to whether it is spoken or written); or one may mean by it these noises or marks as expressive of the mental acts and dispositions which I have been describing. To appeal to 'language' in the former sense is not in the least helpful in showing how ordinary people or scientists may, on the basis of their experience, come to know about a world which exists prior to and independently of their experience. To appeal to 'language' in the latter sense is to be involved precisely in the considerations which I have brought forward.

I have covered a fair expanse of ground in this chapter; evidently I should have said much more about each topic, had I been dealing with it separately and for its own sake. But the object of the exercise was to compare and contrast two accounts of knowledge; and to bring out that while one leads to a host of difficulties and anomalies, as well as to atheism, the other perfectly explains all the relevant facts. The first account is seldom clearly and distinctly set out; when it is, its inadequacies become obvious. Far more often the assumptions underlying it operate as unacknowledged presuppositions, and their tendency to do so has been exacerbated by the hostility in some recent philosophy to the thesis that knowledge has or needs foundations. I have argued that the second account of knowledge is the correct one; in the next chapter I shall examine the contention that it forms the basis for a kind of cosmological argument for the existence of God.

4 Explanation for Intelligibility

The relevance of the foregoing discussion to establishing a case for theism may be summed up in the form of the following two arguments.

A. If the world were not intelligible, it would not be that which we can in principle come to know.
    But the world is that which we can in principle come to know.
    Therefore the world is intelligible.
B. If there were not something analogous to human intelligence in the constitution of the world, the world would not be intelligible.
    But the world is intelligible.
    Therefore there is something analogous to human intelligence in the constitution of the world.

The reader will not be wrong in detecting a studied vagueness in the phrase 'something analogous to human intelligence in the constitution of the world'. Whether, in what circumstances, and with what qualifications, such a being, or collection of beings, might appropriately be called 'God', will have to be determined by further discussion.

It is important to avoid using the term 'world' or 'universe' in such a way as to beg the question of the existence of such a being or beings. If one means by 'the world' 'the totality of what exists', and asks whether there could exist something apart from that totality which provides an explanation of it, the answer must clearly be no.[1] Let us distinguish world (a), the totality of what exists, from world (b) as the totality of what there may be *excluding* God, and world (c) as the totality of what there may be *including* God. In these terms, the question of whether God could not, could, does not, does or must exist, may be put as whether world

(a) could not be, could be, is not, is, or must be identical with world (b); or with world (c). I have already cited Terence Penelhum's claim that the principle of sufficient reason is demonstrably false, since everything cannot be explained.[2] It is true that world (a) and world (c) cannot be explained, because, since the 'world' in these senses consists of everything, there is nothing beside, beyond or apart from it which could explain it. But the question is whether there could or must exist something to explain world (b). The principle of sufficient reason would be satisfied if it could be shown that such a being or beings was or were somehow self-explanatory, in a way in which world (b) is not.

It might be claimed that nothing coherent could be meant by the proposition that the world is intelligible.[3] But its meaning is not in the least difficult to explain. Through the application to our experience of what might be called 'intelligence', by means of which one thinks up possible explanations, and 'reason', by which one considers whether such explanations are probably or certainly correct, we come to know about a world which exists prior to and independently of our experience. Our experience provokes us to ask questions, and to envisage possibilities; we further verify some of the possibilities as being probably or certainly so. These two propositions could hardly be denied by anyone who admits, as the vast majority of people do, both the real existence of an external world, and the real capacity of human beings to come to know something about it. Now a possibility, so far as it is genuine, is intelligible. And when one or more of our hypotheses fail, either in the prosecution of the sciences or in our ordinary affairs, we do not conclude that any effort to explain the world at all is fruitless. We try out a fresh hypothesis. We assume, and cannot but assume, that some hypothesis will turn out to be true of the world; and an unintelligible hypothesis is only a hypothesis at all by courtesy. I infer that we assume, and must assume, that the world is intelligible, in the not very obscure sense that some coherent explanations will turn out to be true of it.

According to N. L. Wilson, 'we cannot conceive of the nonexistence of the world', and therefore 'we cannot significantly wonder why the world exists at all'.[4] But it seems to me that this view is based on a failure to distinguish between what is absolutely impossible on the one hand, and what it is self-destructive for anyone to assert on the other. Certainly, it is to be conceded that the judgement 'There is nothing' or 'There is no world' is self-destructive, in that its truth entails the non-existence of any being with the capacity to assert it. But it may easily be conceived that neither I nor any other being capable of making judgements should have come into existence; and it is difficult to see why just the same thing should not apply to the world as a whole. Whatever the laws and the set of initial conditions on which the cosmos depends, there is no necessity in their being as they are, or even in any such initial conditions and laws obtaining at all; why there should not have failed to be this cosmos, or any cosmos.

What more may be said of the 'something analogous to human intelligence in the constitution of the world'? The intelligibility of the world, it is proposed, is perfectly to be accounted for if the world is due to the *fiat* of an intelligent will which conceives all possible worlds, and wills the one which we actually inhabit. We have a very obvious model of the nature of such a being, and the causal relation he is supposed to have to the world, in the capacity each one of us has to envisage a range of possible states of affairs, and to bring one of them about. Divine creativity is to be conceived on the model of human agency. But where human beings can conceive only a restricted set of possibilities, and bring into being one of a still more restricted set, God is supposed to understand and to be capable of realising all mutually consistent sets of possibilities, and among them all to will to bring about the world which actually exists.

The argument to God's existence which has been suggested is evidently not 'scientific' in the usual sense; indeed, its premiss is the existence of a world such that the sciences are possible. But the structure of the argument is instructively analogous to typical scientific arguments.[5] Like them, it proceeds by advancing an explanation for a given state of affairs; and eliminating rival explanations as inadequate. Among these rival accounts are the following:

(i)   'One ought not to demand explanation of a fact of such generality as the intelligibility of the world.'

(ii)   'Admittedly the world-for-us is to a large extent a mental construction, but it is *human* minds which mould phenomena in the process of coming to understand them; things in themselves might be utterly different.'

(iii) 'The world is not reflected by our consciousness, but is brought into being by it. It is a product of what Hegel would call "Spirit", and our contemporary sociologists of knowledge "society"; belief that the real world exists somehow outside of or prior to these is philosophically or sociologically primitive'.

Briefly, for reasons which can be inferred from what was argued in the last chapter,[6] (i) appears to me to be obscurantist, (ii) plausible but ultimately incoherent, and (iii) grossly implausible and incoherent in the last analysis. (ii) and (iii) are, however, notable as witnesses to the signs of constructive intelligence in the world as we come to know it.

The claim might be objected to that *God* is to be invoked as an explanation for the intelligibility of the world, on the ground that we should always look for 'natural' causes of events and states of affairs. T. R. Miles has argued that failure to adopt this policy is incompatible with a genuine search for knowledge. He says that to classify any event as due to what is 'supernatural' is to imply that the search for natural explanation is in this instance fruitless and ought to be abandoned; and that it is just this assumption which has to be resisted in the interest of scientific advance.[7] Now I would agree with Miles that, at least short of special reason to the contrary, explanation of events is to be sought according to natural causes. Even for the theist, to appeal to divine agency in explanation of why a particular event happened would in most contexts be unhelpful, since, according to him, God is ultimately responsible for all natural events in any case. It would be rather as though a literary critic said, in explanation of some feature of *Macbeth*, 'That was the way Shakespeare wanted it' – so obviously true as not to be informative, and indeed implicitly, in its implication of arbitrariness, as derogatory to God in the one case as to Shakespeare in the other. (It might perhaps amount to a salutary reminder, from the theist's point of view, that a terrible or evil event did not escape God's providential ordering.)

However, once the question is raised of how it comes about that the world is intelligible, or that there is an intelligible world, a 'natural' explanation in the ordinary sense will not do, since it is precisely what is presupposed in the possibility of all 'natural' explanation that the question is about. Furthermore, if it were acknowledged that there was good reason for believing in God, as a result of the asking and answering of this second-order question, why should it not also be allowed that certain conceivable states of affairs would, if they occurred, be more readily explicable as due to an exceptional manner of acting on God's part rather than as an aspect of that ordinary pattern of his activity which is the course of nature? Such, it might be claimed, would be the acts of Jesus, if they were as the four Gospels describe them.[8] And Miles is surely in error in holding that to classify any event as 'supernatural' in *that* sense would necessarily be to *rule out* any attempt at 'natural' explanation; the theist might merely claim that the 'supernatural' explanation appeared best to fit the case, agreeing to abandon it if a 'natural' explanation turned out to be more satisfactory.

Kai Nielsen has observed that, while it is an established and legitimate practice to look for explanations of events within the world, in certain moods we may be inclined to ask what is the explanation for the *totality* of things. But he maintains that this is not really a rational question. 'It only strikes us, or strikes some of us in certain moods, as a rational, literal question because we have an emotional investment, resulting from powerful early conditioning, in so talking about the universe. We should not speak here . . . of an intellectual dissatisfaction, but of an emotional one born of our natural infant helplessness and our early indoctrination.'[9] One may fairly ask, in reply, *why* this is not a rational question. Admittedly it is not rational to ask for an explanation for world (a) or world (c), the absolute totality of what exists, for reasons already given;[10] but this does not imply that one may not properly ask for an explanation of world (b). To put the thing another way, there is no reason why one should not ask whether there is reason to suppose that the absolute totality of things and states of affairs (world (a)) includes that which is related to the rest of it much as the human conscious subject is related to his actions and products. The question becomes more pressing when one adverts to that feature of the world which is so striking in our own times – its susceptibility to scientific explanation. As to Nielsen's suggestions about the psychological factors predisposing people to raise the question, it may reasonably be urged that such factors are involved as much in the intellectual formation of scientists as of religious believers. And one might as plausibly attribute *refusal* to ask the question about the explanation of the world as a whole as due to early-learned responses, or to a revulsion from these, as follow Nielsen in the matter.

As Nielsen sees it, 'that there is no intellectual problem here, but an emotional harassment, felt as a philosophical problem, is evident enough when we reflect that we do not understand what we are asking for when we ask for a non-derivative, non-contingent, infinite being, by reference to which we might contrast ourselves as derivative, contingent or finite beings'.[11] But it is not in the least difficult to determine what we are looking for, at least when the analogy between God and human subjects is grasped. We are asking whether there is evidence for the existence of a being who understands all possibilities, and who effects all those which actually obtain, much as we ourselves choose to bring into effect some among the possibilities which we have envisaged. He is 'non-derivative' in that, while all else is supposed to depend on his will, he is not thus dependent on anything else. He is infinite in that there is no limit to his knowledge, or to what, short of logical inconsistency, he is able to do. He is 'non-contingent' in that he is not liable to come into being or to pass away, whereas all coming into being and passing away depends on his will. Though our own nature as conscious subjects possessed of intelligence and will gives us some conception of his nature, we, as 'derivative', 'contingent' and 'finite', are contrasted with him in all these respects.

One might support the view, that explanation of a fact of such generality as the intelligibility of the world ought not to be demanded, on the ground that such a question is a 'transcendental' one, in the sense that it bears on the very conditions of knowledge rather than on any state of affairs which is to be known. Yet the veto on the question, 'Of what nature must the world be for us to be able to get to know it as we do?', seems at least at first sight as fishy, as redolent of obscurantism, as the veto on any other question. And it is difficult to see how one could go about *justifying* such a veto, without some answer to the question being more or less surreptitiously implied; to the effect that one ought not to ask of what nature the world must be in order for us to get to know it, because the nature of things is *thus*, our knowledge of them is *thus*, and *that* shows why the question cannot be asked. If one does not ask transcendental questions, one is almost bound to make transcendental assumptions. It is perhaps no wonder that philosophers who have considered themselves enemies of metaphysics have tended to oscillate between refusing to answer this question, and giving answers to it which their successors have described and frequently dismissed as metaphysical. One may regard in the same light what Strawson has called the 'disconcerting change of aspect'[12] in Kant's philosophy, between very curious metaphysical doctrines about the interactions of supersensible, non-temporal, non-spatial things-in-themselves',[13] and 'blandly ironical reminders' that questions about such matters are senseless.[14] The fact is that it is a great deal easier to maintain empiricist, idealist or materialist habits of mind, whether one adverts to the fact that one does so or not, than to set out the underlying position clearly and distinctly, and defend it in the face of the objections which may be raised against it.[15] It is a large part of the philosopher's proper business to bring such assumptions to light and subject them to criticism. Only the sceptic is safe, according to Hume;[16] but the sceptic is *not* safe, as was argued above,[17] in that he must rely on intelligence and reason to provide grounds for his scepticism, since if he does not, neither he himself nor anyone else has any reason to take his scepticism seriously. And the principle that one tends to get at the truth about things by applying intelligence and reason to experience is at once subversive of scepticism, and productive of criteria for evaluating more positive philosophical positions and assumptions.

C. B. Martin has distinguished between three types of explanation which we may seek for an event or a state of affairs; 'historical' (that is, through its causes), purposive and theoretical. He remarks of explanations of the second type that they must have a terminus. Thus a man might be said to smash a glass because he wants to attract a waiter's attention, because he wants a meal, because he is hungry, because he is the kind of being in the kind of circumstances that he is. Explanation of the third or 'theoretical' type, he says, would terminate in some ultimate or basic laws of nature, which would hold always and everywhere, and could not be derived from any other laws. Such laws would be logically contingent, and so might conceivably have been other than they are; but 'to ask of an account of how the world is as it is that it should be true by logical necessity is to ask the logically impossible'.[18] Now if such laws *are* really basic, and are admitted to be so, then any attempt to look for an explanation of *them* is necessarily fruitless. Of course, concedes Martin, what is logically compelling may yet be psychologically unsatisfying. I may still feel the urge to frame the question of why these laws are as they are, to seek an explanation of why the ultimate uniformities constitutive of the universe are the way they are rather than otherwise. I may continue to do this 'even though I cannot conceive of what an explanation of this would be like, and even though by my own argument . . . the request for such an explanation is self-contradictory'.

Like a good writer of detective fiction, Martin has provided, in the way he has set out his puzzle, the vital hint as to its proper solution. It is first to be noted that what is basic with respect to the first-order type of question about the explanation of how things are need not be so with regard to questions of the second-order type. In extrapolating from the first-order questions which scientists have asked and answered, one may well come to realise, as Martin points out, that there must be basic laws and initial conditions which are the terminus of this kind of inquiry. But this by no means rules out the possibility that it is reasonable to ask another sort of question, of how there comes to be a world dependent on such initial conditions and laws, and such that human subjects can come to know about it by the application of intelligence and reason to the data of their experience. How this sort of question, once raised, is to be answered, is shown by Martin in the second kind of explanation which he distinguishes. The fact is that we have an excellent idea of what kind of explanation may be found for an intelligible state of affairs which does not have to be as it is, and is not otherwise explicable; the decision of a conscious agent. So there is nothing in the least paradoxical about searching for the explanation of a state of affairs which, while it is 'basic' in terms of the first-order type of question, is not so in terms of the second-order type of question; and there is no difficulty in conceiving what might count as such an explanation.

What is centrally at issue is the curious manner in which the world seems as it were pre-fitted to our intellectual and rational faculties. As was argued in the last chapter, we get to know about the past, other minds, and the fundamental constituents of matter, not just by experience, but by *mental constructions verified in experience*.[19] Yet we do not *create* positrons, or Queen Victoria, or the thoughts and feelings of other persons, out of the data provided by our experience. The world, which we come to know through mental constructions, is thereby full of hints that it is itself a mental construction, but not *our* mental construction. It is not *our* minds which account for the intelligibility of the world, which conformed (approximately) to the laws formulated by Einstein long before Einstein formulated them. Idealists and social relativists forcefully argue, against naive realists, that the world is a mental construction. Theists may go on to point out how implausible it is to suppose that it is *our* mental construction.

In setting out Kant's position on this matter, I shall follow closely the introduction to the second edition of the *Critique of Pure Reason*. The pioneers of natural science, he says, discovered that it is useless, in attempting to acquire knowledge of nature, simply as it were to follow her lead, but that one should on the contrary compel nature to reply to one's questions. This is due to the fact that accidental observations, not made according to any plan, can never yield necessary laws of the kind which it is of the essence of natural science to propound. It is only when experiment is directed according to principles determined by reason in putting forward such laws that it is of any real value.[20] Now metaphysics has not yet achieved the sure method of the natural sciences; instead of making progress, it is characterised by barren and interminable disputes.[21] One might hope to take a hint from the natural sciences, so far as the analogy with them will permit, in attempting to erect metaphysics upon a more satisfactory base.[22]

It has been assumed up to now that our cognitive faculties must conform to the nature of objects; why not try out the supposition that, on the contrary, objects must conform to the nature of our cognitive faculties? Short of this supposition, it must be quite impossible to determine the nature of things *a priori*, quite apart from appeal to experience, as metaphysics attempts to do. But if we make this supposition, there is no difficulty in doing so. 'Understanding has rules which I must presuppose as being in me prior to objects being given to me, and therefore as being *a priori*. They find expression in *a priori* concepts to which all objects of experience necessarily conform'.[23] It follows from this, however, that 'we can know *a priori* of things only what we ourselves put into them'.[24] The things thus to be known are given, and can only be given, in experience. 'We can never transcend the limits of possible experience . . . Our *a priori* knowledge of reason has to do only with appearances, and must leave the thing in itself as indeed real *per se*, but as not known by us.'[25]

These considerations, Kant continues, have the negative significance of warning us that it is fruitless to employ speculative reason beyond the limits of experience. But they have a positive value too, in freeing the practical reason from what impedes its operation and even threatens to destroy it.[26] The important clue here is that things may be taken in two ways, as appearances and as in themselves; this enables the doctrines of nature and of morality each to be confined within its proper limits.[27] Thus man as a phenomenon may confidently be maintained to be subject to the laws of nature, as is a necessary postulate of science; while at the same time, in himself, he may and should be thought of as free and not so subject, as is necessary for morality. Similarly, one may and should hold the morally desirable beliefs that God exists and that the human soul is immortal, while confessing that alleged 'proofs' of these propositions exceed the prerogatives of speculative reason.[28]

The arguments advanced in the last chapter indicate that a kind of *a priori* knowledge, of propositions whose contradictories are self-destructive without being self-contradictory, is to be had of the basic nature and structure both of the human mind and of whatever 'things in themselves' there are, constituting as these do the world which is to be known by human subjects putting questions to their experience. The moral applies, in spite of what Kant claims about 'things-in-themselves', to things prior to and independently of our knowledge of them; short of this, intolerable paradoxes arise in relation to a large proportion of what we are usually supposed to know.[29] And these same aspects of our knowledge make it evident that it is not the things which are to be known,[30] but evidence for the existence and nature of the things which are to be known, that must be given in experience. Our knowledge goes beyond our actual or possible experience; what Kant calls 'speculative reason' ought to explain *how* this can be so, and what can be shown about the nature of things and of the world which they make up from the fact that this is so. Even the basis of our knowledge of God, granted the soundness of my argument so far, may be called 'experience' in rather a wide sense; we can attend to our 'experience' of what it is to come to know, draw conclusions about the overall constitution of the world which is thus to be known, and reasonably postulate the activity of an intelligent will as the best explanation of its having this overall constitution. If one must appeal, as Kant convincingly argues that one must, to the impress of constructive intelligence to account for the nature and structure that the world cannot but have in virtue of being knowable by human beings, and if it must have had this nature and structure prior to being known by human beings, the intelligence concerned cannot be a human one. It may be regretted in some quarters that at this rate one has to forego the advantages claimed by Kant for his dichotomy between 'appearances' and 'things in themselves'; the reconciliation of the demands of morality with the presuppositions and achievements of science will have to be sought along some other route.[31]

To sum the matter up: Kant is right that metaphysics, or the most general possible account of the nature of things, must be grounded in examination of our cognitive faculties; he is also right that such examination results in a system of propositions which are synthetic yet in a sense *a priori*; but he is wrong in inferring that this cannot yield knowledge of 'things-in-themselves', or things as they are and were prior to and apart from our knowledge of them.

I think it would be almost universally agreed by contemporary philosophers that Descartes was wrong in thinking that one had to prove the existence of a truthful God before one could have adequate reasons for believing in the real existence of an external world, or indeed of anything other than oneself.[32] The consensus of philosophers of the present day seems perfectly correct in maintaining, against Descartes, that we have at least as much evidence for asserting the existence of things other than ourselves as of ourselves as thinking beings.[33] Yet it may be inferred from what has been argued here that Descartes was right all the same in seeing a connection between theism and the negation of scepticism. To take our knowledge seriously as knowledge is implicitly to assign a certain overall nature and structure to the world; which is best accounted for if the world owes its existence to an intelligent will such as 'all call God'. We do not have to believe in God to be confident in our knowledge of what exists independently of ourselves; but the fact that we can be confident in our knowledge, and the implications of this fact for the nature and structure of the world, gives us grounds for belief in God.

That the intelligibility of the world is in fact *imposed* upon it in the process of coming to know it, rather than being *discovered* within it, was suggested by Nietzsche, who considered knowledge an expression of the will to power. ' "Will to truth", you who are wisest call that which impels you and fills you with lust? A will to the thinkability of all beings; this *I* call your will. You want to *make* all being thinkable, for you doubt with well-founded suspicion that it is already thinkable. But it shall yield and bend for you. Thus your will wants it. It shall become smooth and serve the spirit as its mirror and reflection.'[34] But it is to be asked whether the suspicion that the world might not be thinkable is or could conceivably be well founded. Even in making the suggestion that the world prior to the thinking of it by the wise might be other than thinkable, Nietzsche must think of what he alleges to be unthinkable. What may underlie the suspicion is a healthy and reasonable scepticism about the claims of any particular theory to represent the final truth about the matters with which it deals, especially when there are signs that it is maintained rather, say, out of reverence for specialist tradition or personal pride on the part of those who formulated it than respect for evidence. But it is one thing to insist that any prevalent explanatory hypothesis should be subjected to critical scrutiny; another altogether to suppose that the whole enterprise of employing our mental capacities to get at the truth about things might itself be mistaken. What could the 'well-founded suspicion' alluded to by Nietzsche amount to? That things in themselves, as they really are, might be utterly different from what could be intelligently conceived and reasonably affirmed on the basis of experience?

It might be complained that the explanation of the intelligible world, as due to the operation of intelligent will, *goes beyond*, in some objectionable way, the state of affairs which is to be explained. But it is characteristic, as I have already argued,[35] of very many arguments in history and the sciences, that they purport to establish the existence of things and the occurrence of states of affairs which are over and above the data which justify belief in them. One goes beyond the data by envisaging a number of competing explanations, and preferring the one which conforms best with the available evidence. In the case of the argument under consideration here, as in these other sorts of case, a state of affairs is adverted to, in this instance the intelligibility of the universe, its amenability to scientific explanation; and a number of possible explanations of this state of affairs are considered, of which one is affirmed as satisfactory, the rest denied as inadequate. If the explanation offered 'goes beyond' what is to be explained in a sense radically different from that in which it does so in these other cases, this has to be shown. It has to be admitted that the argument does differ from an ordinary scientific or historical argument in what one might call its second-order character; in that the *datum* to be explained is not some particular observable state of affairs or collection of states of affairs, but what must be the case about the world for scientific and historical explanations to apply to it at all.

The rejection of empiricism, the doctrine that whatever is or can be known is an object of experience, except where a matter of the meaning of words is at issue, should not be identified with the espousal of materialism. Of course, if for 'materialism' to be true entails no more than that idealism and phenomenalism are both false, and that our beliefs and theories are true or false by virtue of correspondence or lack of correspondence with a reality which exists over and above and independently of them, then I have been arguing incidentally for materialism. But materialism in this sense not only does not exclude the possibility of God's existence, but also, as I have suggested, when its implications are followed through, actually provides reasons for affirming that God exists. From the point of view of a fully critical epistemology, 'matter' is either an actual or potential object of sensation (what can be seen, touched or whatever), or what is intelligible and verified or to be verified as existing by appeal to the senses (like the particles postulated by contemporary physicists, or entities postulated by any future physicists who use scientific method); otherwise it is nothing.

As to the specifically Marxist brand of materialism, John Mepham has usefully and convincingly distinguished two very different conceptions in the work of Marx of the relation of the real world to human ideas about it. According to the first, represented especially by *The German Ideology*, there is on the one hand the real world clearly to be perceived before us, and on the other hand the fog of misleading conceptions which 'ideology' projects between us and it.[36] According to the second, which is that typical of *Capital*, our immediate grasp through our senses of what is directly before us is itself the product of 'ideology'; whereas the real world is to be known in terms of a critical theory which pierces through the veil of appearances.[37] It seems to me that these two accounts of the relation of thought to reality are precisely those which I contrasted in the last chapter. But while it is evident enough that the first account leads to atheism, since God is neither actually perceived nor potentially to be perceived by the senses, it is by no means so obvious that the second one does so.

'Matter', so far as it is real, is something which is to be intelligently conceived and reasonably affirmed by 'mind'; no material process, on the other hand, seems of itself to amount to the conceiving and affirming which are of the essence of mental activity. The 'new materialism' which has recently found favour among professional philosophers inevitably founders, it seems to me, on this fact.[38] It has been suggested that such things as maps provide counter-instances to the thesis that material objects and events cannot of themselves refer to, or be about, other things, in the way that the ideas and judgements produced by minds may be.[39] Plainly the markings on maps are material objects which 'stand for', or 'mean', other material objects; why should not human brains and their parts stand for items in the world in a similar manner? I think that the deficiencies in this view become apparent if one considers by virtue of what it is that a two-dimensional surface with a pattern on it *is* a map, say, of some part of the earth's surface. Mere similarity in shape or structure, however close, between what represents and what is represented, does not seem sufficient. Suppose someone were to smear a handful of birds' droppings on a sheet of white paper, and the result of this operation, by a strange coincidence, were a pattern which corresponded so closely to that made by the streets of the southern half of Leeds that it could be used successfully by a stranger trying to find his way about there. In what circumstances would such a pattern *be* such a map? Not, surely, if it just existed; but if it were either made for such a purpose, or considered as useful for such a purpose subsequent to its making. Material objects or their parts, in fact, can only 'mean' or 'stand for' what is other than themselves by virtue of the intentions of persons. The suggestion might be made that our brains, as sheer material objects, might be maps of the world all the same due to having been made as such, or subsequently deemed to be such, by God or some other person or persons. But I doubt whether such a move to rescue this particular brand of materialism would be much welcomed by its proponents.

It has been suggested that the argument to divine existence from the intelligibility of the world depends on that intelligibility being a *quality*, whereas in fact it is a *relation*.[40] But it may be asked in reply what sort of relation it is supposed to be. Three possibilities suggest themselves. First, the relation may be with intelligent beings within the world. This would imply that there were no things or states of affairs to make up a world before there were intelligent beings in the world for them to be related with; which seems paradoxical in itself (surely there could be a world with no human or other intelligent beings within it?), and certainly runs clean contrary to the assumption of most educated people now that the world existed long before there evolved within it intelligent beings who were capable of knowing it. A second possibility is that the intelligibility of things is a matter of their potential relationship with, that of being understood by, such intelligent beings as might evolve in the world. But if to exist at all is, as I have argued, to have intelligible properties, given that things existed at all prior to the evolution of intelligent beings, they must have had these properties also prior to this. They must *already* have had the properties which made the relationship *possible* – which, of course, is precisely the claim which lies at the basis of the version of the cosmological argument which I am trying to put forward. A third possibility is that the intelligibility of things is a matter of their real dependence on a creative intelligence. This of course is the conclusion of the same argument. However, it is one thing to assert the intelligibility of things, another to say that this is to be accounted for by their dependence on creative intelligence; just as it is one thing to state that the evidence obtains which is supposed to establish some matter of fact, another thing to say that the matter of fact in question is actually so.

Terence Penelhum has pointed out a distinction between two types of argument from the world to God; one demanding an explanation of the bare fact that there is a world, that anything exists; the other of 'the fact, or indefinitely large group of facts, that it contains the particular sorts of quality or relation that it does'.[41] In fact, the argument advanced here seems to amount to a kind of fusion of the sorts of argument which Penelhum distinguishes. Particular properties which happen to be characteristic of things in the world are not at issue; what is at issue is the general property of intelligibility which one might say that things have to have to be things, that the world has to have in order to be a world. A real state of affairs which is not to be intelligently conceived and reasonably affirmed on the basis of the relevant evidence does not seem to amount to a real state of affairs. And it is this very general property which the world cannot but have, if it is to be in principle an object of human knowledge, which, I have argued, is best to be accounted for as due to intelligent will.

One corollary of what we have suggested are the correct synthetic *a priori* assumptions is confidence in the 'hypothetico-deductive method' characteristic of the sciences. It is usual, specially among empiricists, to combine such confidence with denial of such synthetic and *a priori* beliefs. But I do not see how it can be other than a synthetic and *a priori* thesis or assumption that the hypothetico-deductive method applied to experience is capable of providing us with knowledge of a world which would exist, and largely be as it is, whether we had had experience and applied the hypothetico-deductive method to it or not. And such a thesis or assumption seems necessarily involved in any realist account of science. It cannot be analytic, since it *means* one thing for us to perform certain mental operations on our experience, another thing for us to come to know about a world which exists over and above and independently of our experience. On the other hand it could hardly be by experience that we know that a world which exists independently of experience is to be known by application of the hypothetico-deductive method to experience; since it seems impossible to get to know by experience what is presupposed in all cases of getting to know by experience.

Against a form of cosmological argument advanced by Frederick Copleston, Bertrand Russell objected that it depended on grasping the nature of the world as a whole in a manner which was impossible for us.[42] But the upshot of our arguments in this chapter and the last is that we *can* grasp the overall nature of things in very basic outline, and that our successful practice of the sciences depends on the fact that we can do so; and that it is just this basic nature and structure of the world of things, how it cannot but be in order that we may come to know it in the way in which we do, which provides the basis of a cosmological argument for theism. Plato argued paradoxically, but with excellent reasons, that we cannot come to know what we do not in some sense already know;[43] at least we must be in principle capable of recognising the truth before we reach it, if we are ever to recognise it as such when we do so. Could scientists ever have achieved the knowledge of the world which they now have, except on this assumption, which has very seldom been *effectively* doubted — the qualification is important[44] — that the framing of hypotheses and the testing of them against the evidence of experience is the correct method of discovering what is so about the world? And does not the fact that we know *a priori* how to find out about things imply, short of idealism, a certain corresponding nature and structure in things themselves?

It may be claimed that the synthetic and *a priori* principles which I have mentioned should be treated rather as practical injunctions, than as indicative statements about what is the case; and might be expressed rather as follows — 'If you wish to advance in knowledge of the world, pursue the hypothetico-deductive method.' But this does not really dispose of the matter, as can readily be seen if one raises the question of how this practical injunction is to be justified. If it is answered that it is because one actually tends to find out more about the world by following it, then the injunction is certainly justified, but only at the expense of appeal to the very synthetic *a priori* principles which it was invoked to replace. And if such a principle cannot be invoked, the injunction is pointless or misleading; if to follow the injunction is not a means of finding out what is so about the world, why follow it? Someone might urge that it ought to be followed on practical grounds; 'We can build cyclotrons and hydrogen bombs, and put men on the moon, by relying on conclusions reached by the hypothetico-deductive method; what could be better justification than that?' But the claim implicit in the last rhetorical question is ambiguous. Either what is said is irrelevant, or appeal is being made to what amounts to another synthetic and *a priori* principle. The former applies if what the claim amounts to is that since the method is such a successful guide to practice, there is no need to concern onself with the metaphysical question of whether or not it is a means of finding out the truth about things. The latter applies if the claim is rather to the effect that *since* the method leads to successful practice, it is *therefore* a means to knowledge of what would have been the case even if the successful practices had never been carried out.

I have suggested that the susceptibility of the world to being known as a result of questioning by human beings, and more especially its amenability to scientific explanation, implies that it has certain basic overall properties; and that it is reasonable to put what one might call the second-order question of what explanation there is for the features of the world which render it susceptible of explanation. A large part of the problem of establishing whether there is a rational basis for theism is determining the propriety or otherwise of this second-order question.[45]

The apologist for theism is apt to urge that an adequate explanation of things must be one that is complete and total, which leaves nothing still to be explained. But to this it may well be retorted that this is just the sort of explanation which we cannot obtain, and should not expect to be able to obtain. It may be said that the argument that the world as a whole is not self-explanatory, and hence demands an explanation beyond itself, either depends on a wrong idea of the nature and function of explanation, or presupposes an arbitrary re-definition of 'explanation', 'intelligible', and related terms.[46] We know what it is to seek and find the explanation of a thing or state of affairs *within* the world, by reference to other things and states of affairs within it.[47] Why should explanations of another special kind be required?[48] 'Explanation' of the world as a whole, or a 'total' or 'complete' 'explanation' of the things within it, would have to be of this special kind.

It may seem that the apparent force of arguments to God as explanatory of the existence of the world of things, or of certain properties which things possess or may be supposed to possess, depends on 'undermining the tendency to explain the fact singled out by means of more normal explanatory procedures, e.g. scientific ones. The most effective method is to render these *irrelevant* by making the puzzle too *general* for ordinary procedures to solve it.'[49] Ordinary mundane types of explanation, so the story runs, are never complete; so we are inveigled into looking for explanation of another kind. 'The psychological mechanism of this transition is easy to share in, but its rationality is dubious from the start, just because the kind of process we step into is of such a different order from the one we step out of.'[50] Thus it cannot be any kind of *completion* of ordinary processes of explanation. The only reason for accepting the need or possibility of explanation of this special kind would seem to be 'impatience or fatigue'. It may be concluded that 'in the sense in which a Necessary Being explains, contingent causes do not explain incompletely, but are not attempts to explain at all'. And the demand for this very general kind of explanation must be inappropriate, since the only way it could be met would be 'in terms of the logically *im*possible notion of a self-explanatory being'.[51]

In the *Critique of Pure Reason*, Kant speaks of 'ideas of reason', which he says arise inevitably in the course of empirical inquiry, and have the function of setting before us, and stimulating us to pursue, the ideals of unity and completeness in any general type of such inquiry.[52] On Kant's account this ideal, for all that it is unattainable, is one that is proper to hold before ourselves as an incentive. In Strawson's words, 'Illusion is generated only when − as we inevitably do − we mistake the thought of this aim for the thought of an actually existing object of which we may hope to gain knowledge, but only, since it is beyond the reach of experience, by purely rational methods'.[53] Kant thinks of this ideal at most as requiring us, at least as entitling us, to *conceive of* a non-sensible ground of all sensible appearances, which we may envisage as analogous to purposive intelligence; but it does not provide any basis for *knowledge* of such a being.[54] Strawson asks how far it is true, as a matter of fact, that pursuit of scientific explanation is fostered by envisagement of the world as a product of purposive intelligence. He answers, surely correctly, that though it may be so in some minds, it certainly is not so in all.

> The situation cannot be saved by erecting the pursuit of systematic unity in science into a logically sufficient condition of thinking of the natural order as if it were ordained by a divine intelligence outside the world. This would be to sacrifice the doctrine under the pretence of defending it − a procedure adopted by some modern theologians, but not one which enhances the credit of their subject.[55]

The upshot of these considerations is that from the point of view of the interests of reason as such, the postulation of an intelligence directing everything, which provides the 'therefore of every wherefore', seems nothing more than 'the pardonable indulgence of a kind of *fatigue of reason*, a temporary reversion to a primitive and comforting model'. Why should not the ideal of completeness in scientific explanation simply be regarded as autonomous?[56]

Of the points mentioned in the last three paragraphs, it will be convenient to take first the one which was mentioned last. I have myself been arguing that belief that the world is to be known by scientific method can be argued *a priori*; and one may infer from this that the ideal of completeness in scientific explanation is 'autonomous' in the sense of springing from human reason itself. But one cannot validly infer, from the 'autonomy' in this sense of this ideal, the inappropriateness of questions to which the very amenability of the world to this kind of explanation may naturally give rise. Is the world, as it was prior to the discovery of such explanations by human beings, of a nature and structure amenable to such explanations, or is it not? If it is not of such a nature and structure, then, as I have already argued, highly paradoxical conclusions follow for a great deal of what is usually counted as knowledge.[57] If it *is* of such a nature and structure, then it does not immediately appear why one should not seek an explanation of this fact. If someone who is hostile to the asking and answering of this second-order question attributes it to a fatigue of reason, the theist may well retort that failure to ask it amounts to a cop-out of reason. Admittedly the question is not scientific in the usual sense; it could not be so, when what gives rise to it is the very fact that the world is patient of the kind of inquiry which culminates in the sciences. Yet, as I have already argued, it has instructive analogies with scientific questions.[58] And it is certainly not totally different in kind from one kind of explanation which we often look for and get in the ordinary affairs of life; it tends to arrive at the same sort of explanation for the intelligible state of affairs that is the world as a whole as for the intelligible states of affairs which are the actions and productions of human beings. Certainly the answer to this question is ruled out as yielding knowledge, if one insists that, outside the formal systems of logic and mathematics, every object of knowledge must be an object of actual or possible experience. But I have already adduced reasons for thinking that this principle is a spurious one.[59]

Strawson is presumably correct, as a matter of history, about the *de facto* relation between belief in an intelligence directing the universe on the one hand, and the practice of science on the other; that while it may have been fruitful in some minds, it has not been so in others.[60] But the question to be considered here is rather *de jure*; whether the susceptibility of the world to understanding and explanation does or does not provide good reason for supposing it to be the product of something analogous to human intelligence. It may be conceded that it is one thing to *look for* total systematic unity in the explanation of things, another thing to a affirm that there really *is* such a unity, another thing yet to attribute it to creative intelligence; if theistic apologists have blurred these distinctions they have been wrong to do so. This would be, in the terms which I have presented here, to confuse the proposed answer to the second-order question (reasonable affirmation of the existence of a creative intelligence) with the implicit or explicit acknowledgement of the state of affairs (that the world is to be known as, and consequently really is, intelligible and susceptible of explanation) which gives rise to the question. They are on stronger ground if they argue to a creative intelligence, not as though the overall structure implicitly attributed to the world in our confidence of the success of scientific inquiry were a *logically sufficient condition* of this, but as though it *demanded* this as *explanation*. Physicists would not 'enhance the credit of their subject' either, if they stated or implied that the data on which their theories are based were logically sufficient conditions for the truth of those theories, as opposed to demanding (provisionally) the truth of these theories as (at present apparently) the best available explanation of the data.

It might be objected that the type of explanation involved, in terms of the understanding and will of an agent, is primitive and ultimately dispensable. It is notorious that, in spite of the basic correspondence which I have argued for between Aristotle's account of causality and that implicit in modern science,[61] the details of Aristotle's views about causality were largely rejected when modern science was inaugurated in the seventeenth century. At least 'final' and 'exemplary' causes are not now regarded as to be sought in the scientific explanation of natural phenomena; one does not ask for what purpose, or in the partial realisation of what ideal, a lump of sodium behaves as it does when dropped into water, or a piece of litmus paper turns blue when dipped in an alkaline solution. How far the rejection of this form of explanation ought to go is still a matter of dispute. Aristotle thought that the occurrence of X *for* or *with a view to* Y, so that Y is the 'final cause' of X, which is so natural and, at first sight at least, inevitable in explanation of human affairs, applied throughout the universe.[62] God was ultimate in the explanation of things in that while other beings moved or changed with a view of him, he himself existed in changeless self-contemplation. Now Aristotle had a special interest in biology, and it is evident enough that animals and plants seem to operate *for* such ends as the preservation of themselves and their species. It was thus very natural for him to assume that this form of explanation applied to things in general. But after the middle of the nineteenth century, Darwin's theory of evolution by natural selection seemed to show how final causes could in principle be ousted from biology as well as from physics. Similarly, it may be argued, the special form of explanation which we now happen to find indispensable for human actions will prove eliminable when science is sufficiently far advanced.[63]

One might put it that one basic Aristotelian insight, that causes are what one finds out by asking *why* a particular sensible thing exists or state of affairs obtains, but need not themselves be such sensible things or states of affairs, is constitutive of modern science. But the search for 'final' and 'exemplary' causes has not ultimately proved fruitful in physics, has now been eliminated in principle in biology, and may well be held to be on the way out in human psychology as well. Now it may reasonably be said that belief that the universe is ultimately due to an intelligent agent acting for a purpose is of the essence of theism. Thus if the notion of intelligent agency, and the assumptions about final causality which go with it (it is characteristic of agents that they do things in order to realise ends), turn out to have a very restricted application, and even to be eliminable in principle as at worst illusory or at best a mere *façon de parler*, it will be very much the worse for arguments for the existence of God as ultimate explanation for, or cause of, the universe.

Does scientific explanation bid fair to rule out explanation in terms of human agents, their thoughts and purposes? It seems to me that it does not and could not, for the following reason. What reason is there, if any, for accepting the scientific world-view? It seems to me that there is just one excellent reason for accepting it; that is, that intelligent and reasonable human investigators, in a process lasting over several centuries, have come to assert its constituent propositions as a result of testing them, by means of observation and experiment, against their rivals. To do this, they must have deliberately carried out the experiments and made the observations, *in order to* determine whether the propositions in question could be corroborated. But such a process is certainly a matter of human agents acting in accordance with purposes. It may be concluded that, if there is good reason to believe in the truth of the scientific world-view, it is because it has been elaborated and confirmed by human beings acting in a purposeful manner. Thus to rule out explanation in terms of human agents and their purposes is not so much to work out the consequences of the scientific world-view, as to make it impossible for there to be good reason why one should believe in it.

It might be urged that the intelligibility of the world may perfectly well be explained on evolutionary grounds. Given a material world, evolving over thousands of millions of years, would not creatures capable of understanding it tend eventually to come into being, if one grants that such understanding would at least in some circumstances have survival value? Let us concede − I am not at all sure that the concession is justifiable − that *given* an intelligible universe evolving over a sufficient period of time, intelligent beings *would* be liable to evolve in it. This is not relevant to the issue; since what is to be explained is the nature and structure of the world by virtue of which it is *knowable*, which it must have had *before* the arrival of organisms within it actually capable of *knowing* it, and might have had even if such organisms had never come into existence at all. To explain the intelligibility of the world by reference to human intelligence, so far as one admits that an intelligible world existed prior to human intelligence − as I have argued that one must, on pain of intolerable paradoxes[64] − is to put the cart before the horse.

The notion of a self-explanatory being, the postulation of which is somehow explanatory of all else that exists, may well be 'logically impossible' when understood in terms suggested by the ontological argument, where 'self-explanatory being' means or implies 'being assertion of the non-existence of which is a contradiction'. That it is 'logically impossible' when understood in the manner proposed in this chapter does not seem so readily demonstrable. That there should be an intelligent will which is related, *mutatis mutandis*, to the rest of what exists, as the human intelligent will is related to its actions and productions, does not seem an incoherent supposition. If it is objected that human beings are observable, but the supposed divine agent is not, it

may be retorted that human beings *qua* subjects of thought and
will are not observable either, but have to be inferred from what is
observable in the manner already described.[65] And if the objector
goes on to insist that only *some* aspects of real entities may be
unobservable, not *all*, the entities of nuclear physics provide a
counter-example.

According to M. K. Munitz, 'one can . . . affirm that there *is* a
being whose existence, if known completely, would not arouse
any question as to why *it* exists. But such an idea, if not downright
absurd, is, at any rate, opaque to reason.'[66] But it is not at all
clear to me why this should be so. A being which conceived and
willed to exist and occur all else which existed or occurred, rather
as human persons conceive and will states of affairs within their
power, could not arouse any coherent question as to why it
existed. Any such question could only involve appeal to some *other*
being on which *it* was dependent; in which case it would not be
the being on which *everything* else depended for its existence. And
the idea of such a being is by no means opaque to human reason,
since our own nature as beings who, in a very limited way, exercise understanding and will, provides a model for it.

In his *Dissertation* of 1770, Kant argued that God must exist
in order to account for the interrelation of the things which
constitute the world. 'In what principle', he asks, 'does this . . .
relation of all substances rest . . . ? In what manner is it possible
for several substances to be in mutual commerce, and for this
reason to pertain to the same whole?'[67] 'Several substances being
given, the principle of their possible intercommunication is
not apparent from their existence solely, but something else is
required besides from which their mutual relations may be
understood.'[68] It is to be inferred that 'the mundane substances
are beings from another being, not from several, but all from one.
For, suppose them to be caused by several necessary beings: In
intercommunication there are not effects from causes alien to
all mutual relation. Hence the unity in the conjunction of the
substances of the universe is the consequence of the dependence
of all on one.'[69] This conception of Kant's is evidently quite close
to the one set forward here; in accordance with which the interrelation of things would *consist* in their potential relation to an
understanding which had asked and answered all the relevant
questions; and is to be *explained* by their being conceived and
willed together in all their mutual relations. It is of interest,

especially when one remembers Objection 2, that this argument of Kant's, if sound, tends to establish the *unity* of the being on which that aspect of things which he selects for attention depends. What is added to this conception of Kant's in the account given in this book is the analogy between the being postulated on the one hand, and human intelligence on the other (to understand things properly is to understand them not merely piecemeal, but in their mutual relations); this direct analogy with that with which we are immediately acquainted allays somewhat the 'metaphysical' flavour, in the abusive sense of having nothing to do with what is a part of normal human knowledge or experience, of Kant's own conception.

Of course, it is notorious that Kant no longer had any truck with arguments of this kind by the time he wrote the *Critique*. But at least in the *Critique* he is at pains to indicate how there arises in the mind the 'idea of reason' which misleads people into thinking that some kind of knowledge of God, besides that 'faith' based on 'practical reason' which alone is countenanced by Kant, is available to us. One way in which it arises is that natural science may seem to presuppose that nature is due to a supremely wise author, in the manner which has already been alluded to.[70] Another, as Strawson has expressed Kant's point, is that 'the idea of a supremely real being is an idea we are inevitably led to entertain by the commonplace thought of every particular object as having a thoroughly determinate character'.[71] The suggestion amounts to this. Take any object, for example, some particular animal. Its being an animal leaves open a wide range of possibilities as to which species it belongs to; we gain knowledge of this by eliminating all possibilities but one.

> The world, then, is full of determinate individuals, each, as it were, a locus of limitation of all the possibilities which apply to an individual of its kind. The notion of the sum-total of all such possibilities is, therefore, necessarily given with the notion of an actual world of determinate individuals. Kant's suggestion is that we are inevitably led to form the idea of a wholly unlimited superreality corresponding to the sum of all the possibilities which are limited in the case of actual individuals, a reality which we think of as the source or ground of these possibilities, as containing in itself "the whole store of material from which all possible predicates of things are taken".[72]

The idea is not of a collection, but of a single 'preeminently real individual, its individuality corresponding to the unity of things in space and time, its preeminent reality being what makes it the source or ground of all the possibilities presupposed by the determinate characters of actual things'.[73]

Strawson says that it is hard to feel sympathy with the view that the idea of a supremely real being arises naturally in this way.[74] But it may be urged that the case appears in another light once one has demonstrated the falsity of the doctrine that the limits of knowledge are the limits of experience, has made a case for the asking of what we have called the second-order question, and has stressed that the creator so far as we can have any coherent conception of him must be conceived on the analogy of human intelligent agency. An intelligence which grasps the full 'sum of possibilities' (in this sense being 'the whole store of material from which all predicates of things are taken') and wills those which actually obtain in their particularly — this, if the argument of this chapter so far has been on the right lines, is not only a notion which arises naturally in relation to the world in the light of our knowledge of it, but is the most satisfactory explanation of its existence as knowable by us. And once the basic analogy of human intelligent agency is grasped, one can see the force of Kant's suggestion that the idea of a wise author of nature as in a sense presupposed by science is a natural extension of the one just discussed.[75] More or less as human agents do within a very narrow range, God is supposed to determine what is actual within the range of what is possible; this is supposed to account both for how things are in their particularity, and for the amenability of the world to scientific explanation. Such an agent might be claimed to be 'supremely real' simply in that while the reality of all other things and states of affairs depended on him, he himself would not be thus dependent on anything else.

But would such a self-explanatory being be such that its existence could be proved by some form of ontological argument? I do not see why this should be so. An intelligence which conceives and wills the world is to be postulated, on the account put forward here, on the evidence provided by the world; there is nothing self-contradictory about the denial of the existence of such a being. And yet the being might still be 'necessary' rather than 'contingent' in that it could not come into existence or pass out of existence, or be subject to intrinsic change.[76] It might be objected that to argue to God simply on the basis of evidence provided by the world must issue, if successful, in belief in a God who *could not but* have created this world. But this is either to miss the point of the analogy with human agency, or to make some philosophical assumptions which are at best questionable. If I am to account properly for how some artefact, say a flint dagger or a Mozart symphony, was constructed, I must in the long run allude to the intentions and capabilities of the artificer. But my knowledge of his intentions and capabilities need by no means.exclude the possibility that he might have made the thing differently, or even that he might have failed to make it at all. Similarly, if our only evidence, at least of a kind fit to yield knowledge strictly speaking,[77] for the existence and nature of God, is the existence and nature of the world, this does not imply that God had to make a world of just this kind, or indeed any world. Some would urge that the more complete our knowledge of agents, the more we realise that they cannot but do what they do. But this proposition lacks proof, and runs contrary to the universal assumption that agents are often responsible for their actions, and are capable of really initiating courses of action.

The upshot of these remarks is that a cosmological argument of the type which I have been advancing does not need supplementing by an argument of another kind; and the fact is that arguments which have been proposed to supplement it are unsound, and have given it an undeserved reputation for weakness. Having explained the existence of the world by recourse to God, A. C. Ewing asked why God existed; and gave the answer that he did so because it was more valuable for him to do so than not.[78] Now I can understand that, when it is more worthwhile that a state of affairs should obtain than not, there will be some reason to think that it does obtain, *given* the existence of a rational and benevolent agent capable of bringing it about. Thus, if I am uncertain whether or not the inmates of an orphanage are being adequately cared for, I will have grounds for believing this, if I know that the persons responsible for running the orphanage are rational and benevolent, and have funds available for the purpose. But there is no agent capable of bringing God into existence for good reason, or who might fail to bring him into existence, or prevent him from coming into existence, as a result of negligence or malice. Therefore I cannot see why the positive value of God's existence should be accepted as a reason for believing that he exists.

That God exists necessarily, in the sense that the proposition that he does not exist may be found to be incoherent when its implications are fully worked out, has been argued by some from God's status as first or uncaused cause. J. F. Ross has presented a form of this argument, which he derives from the work of Duns Scotus. According to Scotus, what 'can exist but cannot exist *ab alio*', that is, as accounted for by some other thing or things or state or states of affairs, ' . . . is, therefore, a necessary being'.[79] One may summarise the gist of the argument in the following way. That there is an unproducible producer of everything else seems to be logically possible; what is logically possible is either actual or potential; what is potential is producible; therefore the unproducible producer must be actual.[80] The plausibility of this argument is considerably lessened, it seems to me, once one has distinguished between two sorts of possibility. Let us say that a thing or state of affairs is possible$_1$ if there is no incoherence in the conception of it; that it is possible$_2$ if enabling conditions obtain for its existence or occurrence.[81] Why should the existence of an unproducible producer not be as follows: possible$_1$, not possible$_2$, and not actual? Its actuality could be affirmed for good reason only, it seems to me, if it were required to give a satisfactory explanation for some thing or state of affairs which was admitted to exist or to obtain.

The same objection appears to me to apply to the refined version of Anselm's ontological argument which the saint put forward in his reply to Gaunilo.[82] The major premiss of this argument is that if (a) God does not exist and (b) it is possible that God exists, then (c) it is possible that God should begin to exist. But it is not possible that God should begin to exist; that God should begin to exist is incompatible with what is meant by 'God'. Thus it is not the case both that God does not exist, and that it is possible that he exists. But it is possible that God exists, if 'God' is not an incoherent concept. Therefore it is not the case that God does not exist; that is, God exists.

The logic certainly seems impeccable; if there is anything wrong with the argument, it must be that one or more of the premisses is false.

If (a) and (b), then (c).
But not (c).
Therefore not ((a) and (b)).
But (b).
Therefore not (a).

The trouble seems to be with (b), which is ambiguous. Even granted that 'God exists' is coherent — which many modern philosophers have of course doubted — 'it is possible that God exists' is ambiguous, since two senses of possible (at least) may be distinguished. Why should not there be states of affairs which are possible$_1$, without being either possible$_2$ or actual? To put it another way, why should there not be logical possibilities, which are neither actual nor causally possible?

A blend of ontological and cosmological arguments not unlike that proposed by Scotus was put forward by Leibniz. He held that the ontological argument due to Anselm and Descartes was insufficient, since it did not after all show that a necessary being is possible. These philosophers had succeeded in demonstrating, according to Leibniz, that *if* a necessary being is possible, he must exist; but not *that* a necessary being is possible.[83] Leibniz supplemented their reasoning with the argument that unless the necessary being were possible, contingent beings would not be possible either. Since it is plain that there are contingent beings, therefore, and since their reality implies their possibility, the necessary being must be possible. Then, granted what Anselm and Descartes are supposed to have demonstrated, a necessary being exists.

> Those who hold that one can never infer actual existence solely from notions, ideas, definitions, or possible essences . . . deny the possibility of the necessary Being . . . But if the necessary being or *ens a se* is impossible, then all of the things which owe their existence to others will be impossible, since they must ultimately stem from the *ens a se*. Thus no existence at all will be possible . . . If the necessary being does not exist, neither will anything else.[84]

Quite apart from the other objections which may be raised against this argument (of the kind summarised in the second chapter), it is not obvious why the *ens a se* must be identified with a being which is 'necessary' in the sense at issue in the various versions of the ontological argument. And it is difficult to see why mere logical possibility, what we have called possibility$_1$, should require any 'foundation' other than freedom from contradiction. Thus the possibility$_1$ of the existence of chaffinches seems to depend only on the concept of a chaffinch being free from contradiction, not on any real state of affairs at all. However, a great many states of affairs have to obtain for chaffinches to be possible$_2$, for them to have enabling conditions for their existence; animal evolution will have to have proceeded in one direction rather than in others, a certain sort of food supply will have to be relatively abundant, and so on. Why should it not be possible$_1$ that there is an *ens a se*, which is not 'necessary' in the sense at issue in the ontological argument, but which provides enabling conditions for the possibility$_2$ of everything else, while not itself being such that it need have or even could have enabling conditions? Whether there were a universe or not, whether there were a God or not, everything in the universe and a lot besides would have been logically possible; the question is whether God is required for there to be possibilities in some sense stronger than this. Anyone who wishes to argue that there really *is* such a being will have to meet the various objections listed in the second chapter — that the series of causes or enabling conditions might be infinite; that there might be many things which amounted to such enabling conditions without themselves requiring them (that there might be 'brute facts'); and so on; but the ontological argument would have nothing to do with the matter. It appears to me that such plausibility as Leibniz's argument has depends upon a confusion of these two sorts of possibility; it is plausible to say that every object or state of affairs which is possible$_2$, but not that every object or state of affairs which is merely possible$_1$, has real enabling conditions.

That the question 'What is the reason for the existence of the world?' is senseless, and that a positive answer to the question should be given by reference to a being or to beings supposed to be outside the world, plainly do not exhaust the *prima facie* possibilities. There is a mediating position, that, though the question makes sense, we are incapable in principle of finding the answer to it. This has been expounded and defended at length by M. K. Munitz.

It is often claimed, as Munitz says, that all genuine questions are in principle answerable, and that consequently, as Moritz Schlick put it, 'there is no unfathomable mystery in the world'.[85] This view was characteristic of logical positivism, which is now no longer much in favour; but is by no means peculiar to it. Now one may usefully distinguish between three sorts of unanswerable question; those which violate rules of linguistic usage, those which depend on false presuppositions, and those to which there is no known rational method of finding an answer. The proper way of handling questions of the first two types is to point out the flaw involved in the framing of them. (Thus if someone asked, 'What is the square root of Margaret Thatcher?', or 'Who is the tenth son of Margaret Thatcher?', I could point out that one cannot properly use the locution 'square root' in that kind of connection with the locution 'Margaret Thatcher', and that Margaret Thatcher does not in fact have as many as ten sons.) The logical positivist insistence that there must be a rational method for answering questions does provide an effective criterion for identifying questions which are *scientific*; however, 'a definition of what we shall understand by a scientific question . . . cannot rule out the possibility of asking other types of meaningful questions'. The question, 'What is the reason for the existence of the universe?', violates no rule of linguistic usage; and it cannot be shown to be based on an error of fact. But there does not appear to be any rational method of answering it.[86]

Many would of course strenuously deny that we have no method of providing an answer to the question whether there is a reason for the existence of the world. One might hope to find the basis for such a method in common sense, science, religious experience or philosophy. But Munitz argues that none of these is adequate for the purpose. Sense-experience can merely provide us with more information about things within the world; and the rest of what passes for common sense is an amalgam of atavistic prejudices, including strata of more or less antiquated religious, philosophical and scientific thought. Science, too, is exclusively concerned with the understanding of phenomena *within* the world, and hence has no bearing on possible explanations *of* the world as a whole. Also, as already suggested, the theoretical explanations of science are rather subjective constructions than representative of real things or states of affairs existing or obtaining prior to and independently of them.[87] It may be urged that science depends upon the principle of sufficient reason; and that the world itself, like the things and events of which it consists, must have a sufficient reason. Now there is every reason to accept the principle of sufficient reason as a methodological postulate of¹ science; since science cannot abandon it without forfeiting its character as an unremitting search for explanations of phenomena. But it is quite another matter to accept it as a metaphysical principle, applying to a 'fact with which science is in no way concerned, namely the fact that the world exists'.[88]

It is often claimed that religious experience provides people with direct awareness of some supreme being. Now it cannot reasonably be doubted that many persons have undergone and do undergo feelings of awe, dread and fascination; and have accordingly adopted an attitude of worship towards a being supposed to have created the world. But Munitz protests that this by no means goes to show that there really *is* such a being. To say that the feelings concerned constitute a 'faculty of divination', as Rudolf Otto did, is to beg the question. When it comes to philosophy, two possible ways of approaching the question at issue present themselves; that of metaphysical speculation, and that of conceptual analysis. Doubts about the cognitive value of metaphysical speculation have already been raised.[89] As to the method of conceptual analysis, it cannot issue in positive ontological claims. One cannot, as it were, move directly from clarification of the uses of language to propositions about its proper application, except indeed in so far as a question or assumption is exposed as faulty or confused, which cannot be done in this case. Conceptual analysis does tend to bring out that the question is *unanswerable*, on the ground that no means of solving it is available to us; but it does not immediately follow that it is *meaningless*.[90]

Munitz considers the possibility that the reason for the existence of the world might be profitably compared to a conscious and free-acting agent doing something, or bringing about some state of affairs. But he raises the objection that features normally present in such cases, such as a pre-existing material on which the agent works, are lacking in this instance. The consequence is that, however stimulating or entertaining those myths or poetic cosmogonies may be which employ the analogy of human agency to explain the origin of the world, they inevitably founder when taken literally and examined for their validity as so taken. To characterise the world as contingent, moreover, is to say that it might not have existed; and thus implicitly to contrast it with a being which is other than 'contingent', or 'necessary'. But this is to beg the question. In any case, it can be shown that 'the statement "there might not have been a world" is . . . malformed'. To say that what is the case might not have been the case is to imply that what actually took place was one of a set of possibilities. However, this is to refer to a prior state of affairs which is such as to provide the basis for that set of possibilities. But such a state of affairs would itself be a part of the world; thus to say that the world *as a whole* might not have existed is not meaningful. It might be meaningful if it were *assumed* that theism was true; but it is precisely this which has to be established.[91]

One might indeed conclude with good reason that there is no 'reason for the existence of the world', if we meant anything to be conceived on the analogy of types of explanation with which we are familiar in the world. But it does not follow, Munitz maintains, that there might not be a 'reason for the existence of the world' of quite a different kind, so distinctive as to have nothing to do with these ordinary sorts of reason.[92]

I believe that there is a great deal to be said for the logical positivist view that questions make no sense when there is in principle no means of finding out the answers to them. Munitz's admission that the reason for the existence of the world, if there is one, cannot on his premises have anything to do with any normal kind of reason,[93] seems virtually to amount to concession of the point; a reason which has no analogy or likeness to what we would ordinarily think of as a reason sounds suspiciously like no reason at all. But on the basis of the arguments advanced so far in this book,[94] Munitz seems quite right in maintaining, against the logical positivists, that from the fact that a question cannot be settled by methods which are scientific, at least in quite the usual sense of the term, it does not follow that it is meaningless. That the question why the methods of science are appropriate for finding out what is the case about the world *has to be* and *can be* raised and answered[95] is an illustration of the point; one could not use the methods of empirical science to justify the methods of empirical science without begging the question. One has in fact to ask and answer what I have termed a second-order question, in a manner which could not be countenanced on logical positivist principles, in order to justify science itself; once the appropriateness of this kind of question and answer is admitted, there is no great mystery about the right method of answering the question *whether* there is a reason for the existence of the world, and *what* this reason might be. What has to be accounted for is a world which is such as may be known by scientific method, and is therefore intelligible; I have argued that the existence of some being which conceives and wills the world, rather as human agents conceive and will their actions and products, as the best way of accounting for it.

Munitz asks what other kind of reasoning could provide a model for that involved in tackling the question whether there is a reason for the existence of the world; and dismisses in turn common-sense reasoning, scientific reasoning, reasoning on the basis of religious experience, and philosophical reasoning.[96] Certainly the question cannot be tackled by scientific methods in the usual sense; since these methods are applicable, as Munitz quite correctly insists, only to events within the world. The principle of sufficient reason is presupposed in the method of reasoning involved; but, as follows from what I have already argued at length,[97] it is not justifiable to restrict the application of this principle, as Munitz does, to investigations which are scientific in the strict sense. If the explanation of states of affairs by reference to the intentions of agents is to be counted as an aspect of common sense, then it *is* common sense which provides the basis for the kind of reason which we are able to assign for the existence of the world. In this limiting case of agency, it may be urged against Munitz,[98] there is no need to postulate a pre-existing material which has to be worked on by the agent. What applies to agents whose field of activity is a tiny fragment of space and time need not apply to the agent who has absolute disposal of everything within space and time; indeed it cannot do so, since any pre-existing material, being itself in space and time, would itself be due to the conceiving and willing of that being.

In conformity with what I argued in the introduction,[99] it should be conceded to Munitz that religious experience, when taken by itself at least, is insufficient to justify the belief that there is a reason for the existence of the world, and that this is the will of a conscious agent. The arguments which, as I have argued, do justify it, are of a nature which it does seem proper to call 'philosophical', for all that they advert to the presuppositions and achievements of science, and place fundamental reliance, as I have just said, on common-sense modes of reasoning. They include elements of both sorts of philosophical procedure mentioned by Munitz,[100] conceptual analysis and metaphysical construction. The correct system of metaphysics is to be inferred from what it is to come to know, from which may be derived the very basic outline of what there is to be known;[101] to spell out what it is to come to know involves a conceptual analysis of knowledge.[102] For reasons already given at length;[103] such a metaphysics is in the business of stating the truth about things, and not merely of providing, in the manner of metaphysics as conceived by Munitz, an intellectually stimulating or aesthetically appealing approach to the world.

The plausibility of Munitz's claim, that it is senseless to suppose that the universe might not have existed,[104] trades on the ambiguity of the term 'universe'. To apply a distinction suggested earlier,[105] one may distinguish between world (or universe) (a), the totality of what exists, world (b), the totality of what may exist excluding God, and world (c), the totality of what may exist including God. I concede, for the purposes of the present argument, that Munitz may be right in maintaining that to say that some state of affairs might not have been the case is to presuppose the obtaining of a prior state of affairs which left such a possibility open.[106] That it is senseless in consequence to suppose that the world might not have existed, where world (a) or world (c) is concerned, I would also concede, for the reasons given by Munitz;[107] prior states of affairs are presupposed, which would themselves have to be *part of* world (a) or world (c), and therefore could not provide a basis for the possibility of the existence of world (a) or world (c). But there seems no good reason to suppose that the same would apply to world (b); the prior state of affairs in this case could be the existence and intention of an agent capable of bringing it into existence, and these would not themselves be part of that world.

Scientific questions as such are concerned with states of affairs *within* world (b), and cannot be concerned with the existence of that world itself; so far, Munitz is perfectly correct.[108] But he has not shown that a question of a type not strictly speaking scientific, but analogous to this, may not be both raised, and answered by a rational method, about the existence of world (b). And Munitz's view that the claim that the world is 'contingent' presupposes the

existence of a being by contrast with which, as 'necessary', it is contingent, seems simply to be a mistake.[109] That the *idea* of a 'contingent' being, a being which might not have existed, can hardly
be intelligible without the idea of a being, of which it is not the
case that it might not have existed, being also intelligible, is
probably true; but if this were accepted, theism, which implies
the *real existence* of a being necessary in this sense, would by no
means follow. Thus Munitz is wrong in his claim that the question of the truth of theism is begged by talk of contingent being.[110]
And in any case, Munitz himself in effect implies that there both
can be and is a 'necessary being' in the relevant sense, when he
says that it makes no sense to claim that the *world* might not have
existed.[111]

5 Paralipomena

Having set out a form of cosmological argument for the existence of God, I shall consider briefly in the light of it the objections to arguments of this type listed in the second chapter.

It may be true that the causal series as we find it in the world need not be finite; but this is not relevant to the question of whether there may not properly arise another kind of causal question, about the ultimate explanation of the existence of the sort of world in which causal questions of the ordinary kind give rise to real knowledge of things. Even if the infinity of the causal series cannot be ruled out, the impropriety of this second-order kind of causal question does not follow. Similarly, the well-grounded observation that one cannot validly infer, from the premiss that every event or state of affairs has a cause, that there is some one cause which is the cause of every event or state of affairs, is irrelevant to this other kind of causal question.

The suggestion that causal relations may rather be imposed by human understanding on the flux of events which constitutes the world, than discovered as existing in the real world itself, is not in the last resort plausible or even coherent.[1] In fact it is an artefact of empiricism, and short of empiricist claims or assumptions lacks any vestige of justification. Why should we *not* be capable of knowing real causes and causal relations, except, as indeed Hume convincingly showed, on the assumption that every real object of knowledge must be an actual or potential object of experience? But given that the real world is nothing other than what is to be known by the asking and answering of questions about experience, which I have argued must be the truth of the matter, there is simply no problem about the reality of causes and causal relations.

It is an ultimate consequence of our *a priori* assumptions about the nature of the world and of our knowledge of it, which assumptions can be brought to the level of articulate knowledge by dint of inquiry,[2] that there cannot be 'brute facts'. A putative fact which turns out to be incapable of being fitted into any framework of explanation is not a fact at all; it is impossible to spell out what it would be coherently to suppose, let alone to be assured of, the existence of such a 'fact'.[3] The existence of God would not be a 'brute fact' in the sense objected to, since, as postulated in terms of the form of argument advanced here, God, by his nature, is the sort of being whose understanding and will would explain the *how* it is and *that* it is of everything else, without himself being capable of being explained in the same kind of way. That on whose existence, understanding and will the existence of *everything else* depended could not be dependent on the existence of *anything else*.[4]

The argument certainly is a mixture of *a priori* and *a posteriori* elements; that the mixture amounts to a confusion is not obvious.[5] If the drift of what I have said is correct, the same applies to most arguments which purport to establish matters of fact supposed to be the case independently of our experience. *A priori*, the world cannot but be of such a nature and structure that it may come to be known by conscious subjects asking and answering questions about their experience. Then, *a posteriori* — since there does not have to exist the state of affairs which is the world, let alone the human beings who may come to know about it — in the usual manner of causal investigations, one looks for the most satisfactory explanation for the existence and overall nature of such a world.[6]

The claim that what is invoked as explanation cannot be referred to appears to depend on certain assumptions about the nature and preconditions of reference. It might be implied, for example, that I cannot 'refer' strictly speaking to what cannot be an object of my experience.[7] But at this rate, I cannot refer to Julius Caesar, the number three, or the thoughts and feelings of my daughter. If the point is rather that I cannot properly 'refer' to a putative object which is susceptible of no self-consistent description, it has to be shown why the characterisation offered of God is inconsistent, especially when the suggested comparability between divine and human agency, will and intelligence is taken into account. That the world may simply be inexplicable, and that the demand for its explanation as a whole makes no sense, depend respectively on the unanswerability or impropriety of that 'second-order' question, about the nature and explanation of that general state of affairs in which the questioning of experience gives rise to knowledge, which has been considered at length.

'Matter', whenever a coherent account is given of it, turns out to be nothing more than one aspect of the overall state of affairs to which the 'second-order' question applies;[8] since, so far as it is real, it is something which conscious subjects tend intelligently to conceive and reasonably to affirm as a result of questions put to their experience.[9]

If *how* the world is in general is to be accounted for by the divine understanding, *that* it is by the divine will, it may easily be inferred that the overall features of the world alluded to by Thomas Aquinas at the beginning of each of the Five Ways are among the things thus to be accounted for. God is the ultimate explanation of things being brought from merely potential to actual existence, and of their coming into being. He is that imperishable which is the precondition for the existence of all perishable things, and for that of whatever naturally imperishable entities or stuff may exist. If man is, as is usually assumed, superior to other living beings because of his capacity for thought and knowledge, then there is a clear sense in which the unrestrictedly intelligent and almighty will is supreme in excellence, and the source of whatever dignity or value there may be in any other being. Lastly, any inbuilt tendency to harmonious pattern or the realisation of goals that there may be in the universe will be due to him.

With regard to William H. Baumer's objections,[10] it may be said that to conceive of such a being is to conceive of a 'first actuality', 'most being', 'first intelligence', for all that to conceive of him as such is not *ipso facto* to admit *that* he exists. If there exists an intelligent will due to whose *fiat* everything else that exists exists, he supremely exists; but that does not of itself settle the question *whether* he exists. So much for a measure of justification of Aquinas's arguments and conclusions in what I have been saying here. However, in place of the shift of operators often attributed to Aquinas,[11] and of his much-disputed claim that an infinite regress of causes is impossible, I think that the philosophical theist ought to make a clear appeal to the possibility of a 'second-order' causal or explanatory question; since what is at issue is not whether there is a first in the mundane series of causes, but whether there is an explanation for the world having a nature and structure which renders possible the asking and answering of (first-order) causal and explanatory questions.

But the arguments summarised in the second chapter, to the effect that the series of causes going back in time could be infinite, have not gone unchallenged. The case that it could not be infinite was developed particularly by medieval Islamic theologians, and has been expounded and defended in a recent book by William Lane Craig.[12] Aristotle maintained that an actual as opposed to a potential infinite is impossible; and this view was generally followed up to the nineteenth century.[13] (A 'potential' infinite is possible, according to Aristotle, in that one may go on indefinitely adding to an aggregate or dividing a length.) Aristotle believed that the world had always existed, maintaining as he did that the series of past events does not constitute an actual infinite, since its members do not all exist at once.[14] But on Craig's view the fact that the series of past events is in a temporal sequence only adds to the objections against its being infinite. An actual infinite can neither be brought about, nor increased, by the successive addition of individuals. Yet nothing is more obvious than that the series of past events has been formed by the successive addition of individuals, and that it is being added to from moment to moment. And if an infinite number of events had to occur before the present moment arrived, however did it arrive, as plainly it has?[15]

The theorems about the mathematical infinite propounded by Georg Cantor and his successors, according to Craig, have a bearing only on the world of mathematical constructions, and cannot apply to the real world. The supposition that they do apply to it, and that that there could be a real actual infinite, can easily be shown to be untenable by *reductio ad absurdum*. To take Craig's example, let us suppose that the number of books in a library is actually infinite; and that all the books are red or black, with each alternate book the same colour. Would it really be credible in such a case that the number of red books in the library was equal to the number of red books added to the number of black books? But this would be so if the number of books were actually infinite. Again, suppose each of the books has a number printed on it; and that the books with odd numbers are all out on loan. If the number of books were actually infinite, there would be the same number of books in the library after the loans had been made as before. The point might be made that this argument, if it were valid, would make it impossible to attribute infinity to God. But this does not follow, in Craig's view, since God's infinity is not the infinity of an aggregate; 'the infinity of God's being has nothing to do with an actually infinite collection of finite members'.[16]

If the series of events which constitutes the past cannot be an actual infinite, it follows that the world cannot always have existed; and if it has not always existed, it is claimed, then something must have brought it into existence. As Al Ghazali put it, 'Every being which begins has a cause for its beginning; now the world is a being which begins; therefore, it possesses a cause for its beginning.'[17] Those modern philosophers who have attended to this argument are apt to feel dissatisfaction with it; but serious attempts at refutation are hard to come by.[18] I must admit to sharing this feeling of dissatisfaction. However, as other contemporary philosophers do well to remind us, albeit in the slightly different context of attack rather than defence of a form of cosmological argument, a feeling of mental unease about an argument or a position is no substitute for its refutation.[19]

More impressive than these metaphysical arguments, perhaps, is the apparent confirmation by recent scientific investigation of the hypothesis that the universe began to exist a finite time ago. It has been pointed out that the greatest problem about accepting this hypothesis is 'philosophical, perhaps even theological'; if the universe as a whole came into existence at some time in the past, what could have given rise to it? This consideration has apparently given great impetus to the 'steady state' theory proposed as an alternative, in spite of the conflict of the latter with observation.[20] This motive is particularly conspicuous in the work of Fred Hoyle, who says explicitly that the steady state theory, of which he was one of the authors, was devised to bypass the conceptual problems involved in the notion of an origin of the universe.[21] 'The universe is supposed to have begun at this particular time. From where? The usual answer, surely an unsatisfactory one, is: from nothing! The elucidation of this puzzle forms the most important problem of present day astronomy, indeed, one of the most important problems of all science.'[22] Now scientists who maintain that the universe had a beginning commonly do not see this as having any bearing on the question of the existence of God. Craig suggests plausibly that Hoyle, on the contrary, believes that there are theological implications here, and recoils from them. 'To many people this thought-process seems highly satisfactory because a "something" outside physics can be introduced at $t = 0$. By a semantic manoeuvre, the word "something" is then replaced by "god", except that the first letter becomes a capital, God, in order to warn us that we must not carry the enquiry any further.'[23]

Now it appears to me that Hoyle is quite right to insist that it is one thing to claim that the universe began a finite time ago, and that something brought it into existence; another to claim that it was made by a god or God. At least, argument is needed to substantiate the latter claim on the basis of the former. I argued in the last chapter that the explanation for the *existence* of the world, at least in one sense of 'the world', may reasonably be claimed to be the will of an intelligent being; I do not see why exactly the same arguments should not apply to the *coming into existence* of the world, if indeed there is good reason to suppose that the world ever came into existence. Further argument still would be needed to establish that the intelligent being who brought the world into existence is one and the same as the God worshipped by Christians, Muslims or Jews. Suppose that we call the the cause of the origin of the universe G_1, the intelligent agent to whom the existence of the universe is due G_2, and the God worshipped by any representative group of theists G_3. It will not do to take for granted, without argument, that G_1 is identical with G_2 or G_3. But it will not do either to assume that such arguments are bound to fail, in such a way that one can be sure that G_1 is *not* one and the same as G_2 or G_3. It would certainly be obscurantist — this seems to be the basis of Craig's and Jaki's complaints about the theological motivation of many who reject belief in the 'big bang' — to repudiate that hypothesis on the ground that it would lead to belief in the existence of G_1, which in turn might very well turn out to be probably or possibly identical with G_2 or G_3. Hoyle's other suggestion, that to ascribe the big bang to God is to warn that inquiry may be taken no further, can be given shorter shrift, for reasons suggested earlier.[24] Why should this be so? Why should it not be claimed that reason and experience at present confirm the hypothesis that some event of the past was due to the direct (primary) causality of God rather than to any derivative (secondary) cause or causes; while it is yet admitted that further evidence or further inquiry might provide good reasons for rejecting the hypothesis?

It might be asked what relevance, if any, evidence that the world came into existence a finite time ago has to the principal argument of this book. Evidently the relevance is at best indirect;

the world is intelligible, and its intelligibility demands explanation – if the argument is sound – whether or not the world has always existed. Yet it may be urged that in the case of an event for which (a) there are no 'secondary causes', or causes amenable to the usual kind of scientific investigation, to be invoked – and this is of the essence of the big bang – and (b) it seems arbitrary to deny causality of a kind, the existence and activity of the 'first cause' obtrude themselves more on human speculation and belief than they are otherwise apt to do.[25]

But it is obvious that, whatever be the ultimate verdict of the learned world on the big bang, the position for which I have been arguing implies a strong compatibility between theistic belief on the one hand and the methods and results of science on the other. This of course runs clean contrary to what has been a very widely held assumption at least since the middle of the last century; that science and theistic belief are in the last resort incompatible. In the last few years, the view that they are not only compatible, but that theism leads naturally and more or less inevitably to the development of science, has gained ground among historians and methodologists of science; Rolf Gruner has given those who maintain this view the convenient label of 'revisionists'.[26] Judeo-Christian theism, the revisionists argue, is in fact the prime cause of the development of science; this provides the answer to a question which has preoccupied many historians, of why science developed in European Christendom, and not in any of the other civilisations – such as the Chinese and Meso-American – which were at least equally sophisticated in other respects, and had a highly-developed technology. The revisionists further point out that many hints that the sciences can be and ought to be pursued are to be found in the Judeo-Christian Scriptures.[27]

An obvious objection to this thesis is that, while Christianity dominated European thinking from the fall of the Roman Empire onwards, modern science did not really get going until the seventeenth century. If Christian theism is really so significant a factor in the emergence of science, how is this very considerable time-lag to be accounted for? As the revisionists see it, Christian thinking up to the seventeenth century was hamstrung by alien metaphysical conceptions of Greek origin, which culminated in the system of Aristotle as championed by the Roman Catholic Church; this prevented the unprejudiced and unfettered investigation of things by its *a priori* assumptions. (It has been pointed out that most representative revisionists are Protestant.[28])

In his article criticising revisionism, Rolf Gruner does not advocate a return to the older account against which the revisionists were reacting. However, he does provide a number of reasons for considering that their reaction was excessive. The Bible, as he points out, contains at least as much support for the belief that scrutiny by man of God's works in nature is a wicked blasphemy, as for the conviction that it is in accordance with the Creator's will. Also, there is no denying that the opponents of Christianity have persistently used science as a stick with which to beat it; surely they would not have done so, either for so long or with so much success, if they did not have at least a *prima facie* case. Furthermore, when it comes to the revisionist critique of Hellenism, Christian contemplation of the glory of God on the one hand, and speculation in the Greek manner on the ultimate reasons for things, have far more in common with one another than the revisionists allow; and both are equally far removed from the whole tenor of modern scientific investigation, where the fundamental aim is not to contemplate nature, but to subdue it and make it conform to human ends. The fact that the word 'theory', which is used to designate a crucial aspect of science, is derived from the Greek 'theoria' or contemplation, is a mere coincidence; there is really nothing in common between the types of mental activity involved.[29]

My own principal difficulty with revisionism is by no means the same as Gruner's. I think that both Gruner and the revisionists mistake the significance of Greek metaphysics, and in particular the work of Aristotle, at once for Judeo-Christian theism and for science. The revisionists, as Gruner remarks, tend to follow the lead of Francis Bacon on this matter.[30] Bacon lambasted Aristotelianism in the name both of science and of religion. Metaphysics of this type, he maintained, amounted to a blasphemous attempt by man to impose upon nature the forms of his own thought; to observe and to experiment without such presuppositions was at once the most effective means to knowledge and mastery of nature, and a matter of pious submission to God.[31]

In the philosophy of science of the last few decades, the reaction against this aspect of Bacon's work has been pretty fundamental;

the role of theory and hypothesis in science has been stressed, and the notion that we can, let alone ought to, inspect nature as it were with rinsed eyes, without any presuppositions, has been subjected to very damaging criticism. Whatever the disagreements, for example, between Popper, Kuhn and Feyerabend, they are at one in this. What I find rather surprising is that more credit has not gone to Aristotle as a result of this change of view. If my own arguments earlier in the book are on the right lines, one may well infer that, of all ancient thinkers, Aristotle hit off most judiciously the manner in which constructive intelligence on the one hand, and experience on the other, co-operate in our pursuit of the truth about the world. Plato had made a radical contrast between the sensible material world on the one hand, and the noetic heaven of 'forms' on the other. But Aristotle insisted that the real world, including the 'forms', was to be known by asking such questions as 'What is X? Why is this an X? Why does X exist?', with respect to observable things and states of affairs.[32] Surely, in this respect at least, modern science, so far from being anti-Aristotelian, is a resounding illustration and vindication of Aristotle's position. As it is now it is the result of a persistent effort, over many generations, to find out the nature of observable things, and why observable states of affairs turn out in the way they do.

Bacon's chief complaint against what he calls the 'Rationalist' school, of which Aristotle was the chief representative, is that it 'snatches from experience a variety of common instances, neither duly ascertained nor diligently examined and weighed, and leaves all the rest to meditation and agitation of wit'.[33] While this may well be a reasonable charge to bring against the method of Aristotle as set out by him in detail,[34] and *a fortiori* against that both propounded and implemented by later Aristotelians,[35] it does not seem to touch Aristotle's initial claim that the world is to be known by two kinds of question addressed to the things and states of affairs of our experience. Bacon in effect supplements that claim by a reminder that the judgements which one arrives at as a result of such questioning ought rigorously to be tested through observation and experiment. Still, the 'meditation and agitation of wit' involved in questioning, in the propounding of hypotheses, and in the thinking-out of suitable tests for the hypotheses, remain, quite apart from the making of observations, an absolutely necessary component of science. Science gets nowhere, however assiduous the investigator is in looking about him and gathering observable data, short of the *a priori* assumption that the real world is nothing other than what is to be known by the asking and answering of questions about those data. Bacon's maxims are an extremely useful corrective to an abuse — in the terms employed earlier,[36] that of underestimating attentiveness at the expense of intelligence and reasonableness; but taken literally and seriously as normative for science in general, as modern philosophers and historians have shown *ad nauseum*, they would have been fatal to it.

What is the bearing of this discussion on belief in God? Christian and other theists regard the world as a product of intelligent will. As M. B. Foster (an author cited as revisionist by Gruner) suggests, some aspects of science in effect lay emphasis on the signs of divine intelligence, others on the signs of divine will, in the world.[37] That the world is amenable to theoretical explanation at all depends on its intelligibility; but every proposed theoretical explanation has to be verified by observation and experiment. Bacon's point against Aristotle and the Aristotelians amounts to a stress on the latter fact at the expense of the former. That most of the revisionists are, as Gruner remarks, Protestant, is perhaps no coincidence, as it was of the essence of early Protestantism to stress the sheer will of God at the expense of his providential ordering of things so far as these can be traced by the use of reason independently of special revelation.

That there is an extraordinary intellectual delight to be had in coming to understand natural phenomena is something which I should have thought would be agreed upon by most men of science. It seems to follow from this that Gruner is simply wrong in denying that *theoria* or contemplation has anything to do with scientific theory. Is it not to a large extent this intellectual delight which is the pay-off for the real scientist, as opposed to the technologist or the academic social climber? Gruner's opinion that science is not to be regarded primarily in this way, but rather as a means of manipulating our environment, appears to me a dangerous aberration.[38] It is just this conception of science as primarily a means to technology, together with the actual abuses of technology, which has been primarily responsible for that tarnishing of the reputation of science in the last few years which is remarked upon by Gruner. If only science were seen primarily in terms of *theoria,* of intellectual delight in the understanding of the world, rather than merely as a means to technology, I think that the contemporary fashion which opposes science, and which seems to me both dangerous and deplorable, would not be as widespread as it is.

The revisionists oppose theism and science to Aristotelianism, whereas Gruner opposes Aristotelianism and theism to science. It is the upshot of the argument of this book that all three are *de jure* if not *de facto* closely allied, a revised Aristotelianism[39] as the correct overall (metaphysical) account of the real world to be known by inquiry into the states of affairs given to our experience, science as the active and detailed prosecution of such an inquiry, and theism as the most satisfactory way of accounting for the existence and nature of a world which is to be known by such inquiry.

It must be admitted that Gruner has the basis for a *prima facie* case against both the revisionist view and the one which I have argued for, in the actual conflict which there has been between science and theistic religion. The conflict appears to me to be due to a number of factors. First, there is the assumption that the presuppositions or implications of science are empiricist or materialist, and that materialism and empiricism are both incompatible with belief in God. While the latter is certainly true, I have tried to show at some length that the former is false. Second, there is the notion that God is not known in and through the intelligibility of the universe, but rather through whatever aspects of it there may be which are unintelligible; on this 'God of the gaps' view, the further scientific explanation advances, the less reason there is for belief in God. The whole thrust of the argument of this book is evidently in radical opposition to this conception of God. Third, there is the striking divergence between the findings of ancient historians and palaeontologists on the one hand, and on the other what appears to be the plain meaning of a number of the statements in the Scripture which purports to contain the revelation of God. This is a somewhat complex and difficult issue, into which this is not the place to go; it is not directly relevant to the question considered in this book, whether the existence or nature of the world gives any good reason to think that it is due to intelligent will.[40] Fourth, there is the conviction which has quite frequently prevailed in the history of Christianity, that man is a being so sinful and contemptible that he ought to abase himself before God, rather than blasphemously exerting his mind and his will to know and to change the material world and society. To this may be opposed a very different account, that true obedience to God consists in the cultivation of his image in man, that is, in the strenuous exercise of intelligence and reason to know what is true and good, and of the will to act accordingly, in opposition to all the temptations to selfishness and self-deception which arise from our individual situations and the social groups to which we belong.

If this account is on the right lines, it may easily be seen that, in spite of many unfortunate episodes in the history of the relations between theism and science, there is a fundamental similarity of interest and intention between them. Science is a matter of being unrestrictedly attentive, intelligent and reasonable in relation to the data bearing on the nature of the external world;[41] Christian sanctity is largely a matter of being unrestrictedly attentive, intelligent and reasonable in relation to the data bearing on the person's own moral character, and that of the groups of which he is a member. The saint would have a great deal in common with Sir Karl Popper's exemplary scientist; being prepared to undergo 'the way of the cross' in testing against the evidence especially those judgements about himself and his group which he and his group find most gratifying to their self-esteem.[42] Sinful human pride is a matter not of the excessive use of intelligence, but, on the contrary, of premature contentment with the results of its efforts, and of failure to supplement these by the use of attentiveness and reason; and in any case one is not the more intelligent as a result of being the less attentive or reasonable.

*   *   *

The objection to talking about 'the world' or 'the universe' as a whole in the context of the cosmological argument has not been left without some answer by reflective theists. Richard Taylor protests that the fact that the world is a very big object is no proper objection to the claim that the same general causal questions arise about it as about other objects. No particular thing or state of affairs *in* the world need have existed; and there seems no more reason why this particular totality of things and states of affairs (the actual world), or any other such totality, need have existed. It would be odd to insist that nothing in the world is a mere accident, or simply derives its existence from itself alone, while denying that the same applied to the world itself. How long the world has existed, or whether it came into existence at any time in the past, does not affect the issue. Even if it had no beginning, it still makes sense to ask why there is a world without a beginning — meaning by 'the world' 'the totality of all things except God, in case there is a god'.[43]

Similar points are made by Peter Geach. There is no difficulty, he admits, in holding that the series of causes in the ordinary sense goes back to infinity. The kind of causal argument which may reasonably be used in support of theism involves 'something tantamount to treating the world as a great big object. And it is natural to regard it thus — as the upper limit of the series: Earth, solar system, galaxy, cluster of galaxies . . . If the world is an object, it again seems natural to ask about it the sort of causal questions which would be legitimate about its parts. If it began to exist, what brought it into existence? In any case, what keeps it from perishing, as some of its parts perish? And what keeps its processes going? And to what end?' It is merely childish to object that the world is too big for these sorts of question to be legitimate about it; and 'to say the world is all inclusive would be to beg the question — God would not be included in the world'. And there is no need to be embarrassed by the question, if it is reasonable to ask who made the world, why is it not reasonable to ask who made God. 'For the world shares with its parts certain attributes that give rise to causal questions: it is a complex whole of parts and is in process of change.' But, as the theist is liable to maintain, 'God is not a whole of parts and is unchangeable; so the same causal questions need not arise about him'.

The reasons for philosophical discomfort in talking about 'the world' as a whole, it seems to me, arise partly from distaste for theism — one seldom hears such objections made to claims like 'hydrogen is the commonest element in the universe as a whole' — and partly from the ambiguities in the meaning of the expression 'the world' mentioned in the last chapter.[44] But in the light of the distinctions drawn at that point, one may understand the point of view of both sets of disputants on this issue — those who maintain that one may not legitimately treat the world as a whole as an object, in such a way as to ask causal questions about it; and those who maintain that one may do so. The former party is right so far as there are senses of the term 'the world' in which causal questions cannot arise about it at all; the latter party is right so far as causal questions of a second-order type do arise about 'the world', at least in one sense of the term.

6 Conclusion

In conclusion, it seems worthwhile to disentangle, and briefly to set out, the salient features of the argument of this book. They are:-

(1) that knowledge is possible;
(2) that the world is nothing other than what knowledge, actual or potential, is of;
(3) that the world's capacity to be known entails something about its overall nature and structure;
(4) that the fact that it has such an overall nature and structure is best accounted for on the supposition that it is due to the *fiat* of some one entity analogous to the human mind; which is roughly what is commonly meant by 'God'.

As to proposition (1), denial that knowledge is possible disposes of itself. If it were at once true, and based upon good reasons, it would itself amount to an item of knowledge, and so would falsify itself. If there are no good reasons for propounding it, on the other hand, it may be dismissed from serious consideration.

The vindication of proposition (2) may be inferred from the well-known incoherence of Kant's conception of the thing-in-itself, which is neither an actual or potential object of our senses, nor to be known through intelligent and reasonable inquiry into what is given or available to our senses.

Against proposition (3), it is liable to be objected that one cannot make a statement of such generality about the nature of the world. But it may be answered that a proposition of such generality is stated or implied by any justification or explication of any proposed method of finding out how things are in the world, including that of science.

When it comes to proposition (4), there is nothing in the least unusual about the *kind* of argument that is needed to support it; it is just the same in principle – the suggestion of possible explana-

118

tions of acknowledged states of affairs followed by elimination of unsatisfactory ones – as that used to determine any matter of fact. The argument differs from other similar arguments only in the extreme generality of the state of affairs – the knowability and intelligibility of the world at large – which is to be explained.

On a superficial view of the conception of the world advanced in this book, it would appear to be idealist. To a more attentive view, on the contrary, it turns out to be the only alternative to idealism, given that materialism turns out to be fatally ambiguous, common-sense realism to be mistaken, and empiricism to be incoherent. The basic structure of the world is not due to our minds; but it is and cannot but be due to something analogous to our minds.

Appendix • A. J. Ayer on Metaphysics and Theology

I have been arguing in this book that attention to the nature of our knowledge of the world, and how we build it up from our experience, provides grounds for affirming that God exists. Sir Alfred Ayer's *The Central Questions of Philosophy*[1] sets out rather a different account of our cognitive relation to the world, and draws atheistic conclusions from it. Ayer is among the most distinguished and influential of contemporary philosophers, so it seems worthwhile to examine his arguments and conclusions in the light of what I have claimed.[2]

In discussing the verification principle, Ayer distinguishes between those versions of it which require that the content of a meaningful non-analytic statement should be reducible to that of the statements reporting direct experience which might verify it, and those which do not. He remarks, in my view very justly, that the difference comes out with especial clarity in the case of historical propositions;[3] versions of the former set would commit one to the remarkable thesis that all that is *meant* by statements about the past is that certain observations would be made in certain circumstances in the present or the future – a view which 'no longer seems to me', as he puts it, 'to be tenable'. As applied to science, he thinks, the former set of versions has the merit of getting rid of 'occult properties' in things; to speak of electrical currents, for example, would be no more than a commodious way of saying that in certain circumstances bells will ring, engines run, people suffer shocks, and so on. However, as he says, it does not appear that one exhausts the meaning of a scientific theory by however wide a specification of its observable implications as known at any particular time.[4]

A more satisfying solution is thus to regard the sum total of propositions of observable fact as together constituting what may be called (following F. P. Ramsey) the 'primary system', and to

120

contrast this with a 'secondary system' concerned with the arrangement of facts. The distinction between fact and theory is vague, and we have some choice as to where to draw it; still, a reasonable decision can be made on the matter. It seems proper that any proposed metaphysical theory of the nature of things should be required 'to function as a secondary system, at least to the extent of having some explanatory value'. It may be asked why this requirement should be made; and whether it does not turn out to be a mere stipulation, which there is no need for anyone to comply with if it does not suit him to do so. 'To this I can reply only by asking what interest the theory could have otherwise. If it does not aspire to truth, we need not worry . . . But if the theory does aspire to truth, there should be some way of deciding whether it attains it' − if not by way of factual content, then in arrangement of the facts. One may complain that this is to beg the question; but 'what are the alternatives against which it is begged?'[5]

Our ordinary judgements of perception in a sense go beyond the evidence; 'they claim more than is strictly vouchsafed by the experiences which give rise to them'. How do we come in each case to make such a claim, and how is it justified? The percepts presented to any one observer, or even to all observers that there have ever been, simply do not add up to our conception of the physical world. To speak at all adequately of that world, or indeed of any of the material objects of which it consists, in terms of percepts, one has to allude to possible as well as actual percepts; and most of the propositions setting out such an account of the world will be unfulfilled conditionals. (Thus, if I am speaking of a state of affairs at which no sentient being is present, I have to say that *had* such a being been present in the right conditions, he *would* have enjoyed such percepts.) In opposition to his own earlier views, Ayer now thinks that such conditional statements should belong to the 'secondary system' already described; which has an explanatory function in relation to the 'primary system' of 'purely factual propositions'. At this rate 'they are not themselves equipped to function as primary statements of fact'. The passage from percepts to physical objects is not to be treated, owing to the difficulties already mentioned, as a matter, strictly speaking, of logical construction (as would be possible if statements about physical objects were reducible in meaning without remainder to statements about percepts), but rather, in the manner of Hume, as a matter of imagination. For Ayer, as for Hume, it is the 'constancy and coherence' of our percepts which give rise to belief in a comparatively stable world; but they differ in that while for Hume we are deceived into thinking that there are persistent objects, for Ayer this is justified as an acceptable theory. 'The continued and distinct existence, not of percepts, but of the objects into which they are transmuted, is simply posited. *Consequently,*[6] we are able to forsake phenomenalism for a sophisticated form of realism'.[7]

Still, it is one thing to believe that things exist when not being perceived; another thing to hold that they actually have the properties which common sense would attribute to them on the basis of perception. That the properties which things appear to have are not the properties which they really have, but that the appearances are caused by the real properties, has often been maintained on scientific grounds. Ayer admits that on his view there is a difficult problem of whether the properties which things really have, independently of our perceiving them, are a selection from among the properties which they appear to have, or whether they are quite different. The trouble with the latter view, he thinks, is 'that the unobservable entities which are *sometimes* admitted into physical theories gain credit from their relation to objects which are thought to be observable' (italics added). If physical objects were really unobservable, we should have no means of identifying them, and so no reason to believe that they played any part in the causation of our percepts, or even that they existed. And it may well be inferred, from the fact that scientific theories belong to the 'secondary system', that the unobservable entities which figure in them, so far from being ultimate constituents of the real world, are nothing but conceptual tools. In the long run, the issue between a pragmatist and a realist view of such unobservable entities is a matter for decision. If it seems curious not to treat the question of what there really is as a question of fact, one can only answer 'that if the problem were treated in that way, we should have no procedure for solving it'. Ayer himself is inclined to the view that fundamental particles are parts of observable objects, imperceptible not as it were essentially, but due to their being so small. Such an account of them has the advantage that it 'makes some concession to scientific orthodoxy, without doing any great violence to the more simple theory' of common sense 'which is naturally developed out of our experiences'.[8]

In the course of considering a number of conceptions of metaphysics, Ayer speaks of one view of it as a competitor of natural
science, purporting to deal with the underlying reality while
science deals only with the appearances. He says that the main
difficulty with this view is that of making it intelligible. While we
are used, he points out, to the idea that appearances can be de-
ceptive, this turns out to be a matter of the conflict of the appearances with one another rather than between the appearances and
something of an altogether different kind. 'What possible experience could authorise our making a distinction between appearances as a whole and a quite different reality?'[9] In any case, 'it is
vain to attempt to dissociate the world as it is in itself from the
world as we conceive it'.[10] This last seems to me true and important in one sense, quite false in another. It all depends who 'we'
are, and how broadly the 'conceiving' is conceived. The fact is
that the 'experience', in rather a broad sense, of pursuing the
natural sciences, and reflecting on this pursuit, *does* at first sight at
least authorise just such a distinction between appearances as a
whole and reality as a whole, between the world as it really is and
the world as it might be comparatively ignorantly or unreflect-
ingly conceived. By dint of inquiry, observation and experiment,
we come to know of the real world in terms of a conceptual apparatus very different from that of common sense, whose elements
by no means directly correspond with what appears to our senses,
and which are at least widely supposed to represent the nature of
things as they really are. If the task of the sciences is to achieve
such an explanatory account of the world in detail, this leaves to
metaphysics the business of discerning of what overall nature the
world must be in order to be susceptible of being known in this
kind of way. At this rate, of course, metaphysics, so far from
being a rival to the sciences, would be complementary to them.
Such a metaphysics would in its way meet Ayer's requirement of
being part of the 'secondary system' whose function is to explain
the primary facts.

Ayer's arguments and conclusions seem strongly redolent of
compromise, influenced as they are by the need to maintain experience as the touchstone of reality, along with the desire not to
offend against the canons of common sense or of science. He
seems perpetually to hover between the empiricist view that the
real is an actual or at least potential object of experience, and
the alternative view, which I have argued is the correct one, that

the real is what is to be intelligently conceived and reasonably affirmed as the explanation of what is available to experience. His indecision comes out in a specially striking way in his discussion of his 'secondary system' of explanatory concepts and theories. As I have said, on his view, the question of whether, and if so how far, the postulates of the 'secondary system' correspond to things as they really are is unanswerable except by sheer decision.[11] An unsympathetic critic might maintain that a firm decision either way on this issue would have unfortunate consequences for Ayer. To insist that what is real can only be what belongs to the 'primary system' is to make mincemeat of the scientific realism by which Ayer is, in spite of many of his principles, attracted; it is also to be compelled to those highly paradoxical conclusions about the nature of historical propositions which Ayer once held, but now claims, though significantly he gives no reason, to have abandoned.[12] Ayer's concession that unobservable entities are 'sometimes' admitted into physical theories[13] seems excessively coy; I would have thought that the wholesale commitment by theoretical science to the existence of unobservable entities is obvious enough, however little it suits an empiricist who sets store by scientific respectability to acknowledge the fact. If one acknowledges that entities postulated within the 'secondary system' may belong to the real world, so far as they are required as providing explanation or sufficient reason for what is observable (in accordance with what I have argued to be the correct account), and develops this position consistently, the upshot will be the abandonment of empiricism.

There are at least two senses in which entities may be said to be 'occult'; that they are not perceptible, and that their existence is not verifiable by reference to what is perceptible. I agree with Ayer that talk of entities of the latter kind has no place in a true account of the nature of things;[14] but one cannot get rid of talk of entities of the former kind without getting rid of science, history and common sense. Ayer's admission, that even our ordinary judgements of perception 'claim more than is strictly vouchsafed by the experiences which give rise to them',[15] seems to me to be crucial. How are such claims ever to be justified, on his view? He suggests that we should follow Hume in saying that the order in and between our perceptions causes us to imagine a relatively stable world of physical objects; but not accept Hume's sceptical conclusions about our right to say that the latter actually exists.[16] But it seems to me that a mere *posit* of the existence of such a world of objects is insufficient to *constitute*, let alone to *justify*, a 'sophisticated form of realism' as opposed to a mere phenomenalism or pragmatism. Frankly, fideism seems to me no more satisfactory a stance in relation to common-sense realism than in relation to theistic religion. Of course, if a consistently critical realism is adopted, Ayer's difficulties in justifying belief in relatively stable and continuous physical objects simply disappears. Objects of judgement (including ordinary physical objects) are sharply to be distinguished from direct objects of sensation (what Ayer calls 'percepts'); real things, on pain of the self-destructiveness of judgement, are what true judgements are about; some of our intermittent sensations give us excellent reason to believe in continuous objects, which exist when no sensations of them are being enjoyed. [17]

Against the thesis that objects are really characterised exclusively by imperceptible properties, Ayer raises the interesting objection that on this view we would have no means of identifying objects; and thus would 'have no reason to believe that they played any part in the production of our sensations, or even that they existed at all'. [18] The solution to this puzzle is that it is the same objects which are to be known in an elementary way, and identified, in terms of their perceptible properties; and which are to be known as they really are, in terms of properties and relations which are not themselves perceptible, but are to be reasonably affirmed to exist as a result of inquiry into what is perceptible. For example, mass in the scientific sense is not directly perceptible; but the success of the law relating force, mass and acceleration in explaining and predicting phenomena is a strong indication that mass in this sense really characterises material things.

It will be remembered that it is the basic argument of this book that the existence of a world, with certain very general features which ours has, is best accounted for if it is held to be due to something analogous to human intelligent will. That it has these very general features is a matter not of its being entirely observable, even in principle, but of its being knowable through questions put to observation. Ayer's conception of the world seems to be an unstable compromise between these conceptions; his empiricism and loyalty to Hume pulling him in the direction of the first, his respect for science and for common sense inclining him towards the second. The first, as I have argued at length, leads to very

paradoxical conclusions; the second confirms the basic intuitions
of common sense and scientific realism, but leads out of empiricism. Ayer, in fact, neither unequivocally sticks to empiricism,
nor wholeheartedly affirms the position about the nature and
structure of the world which I have argued leads to theism by way
of a hypothetico-deductive argument; but compromises at the
cost of vacillation and indecision on a number of central philosophical issues.

Ayer's treatment of the claim that it is reasonable to believe
that there is a God has next to be considered. First, as he says, one
has to establish roughly what is meant by 'God'. Those who believe in one God generally maintain that he is something like an
intelligent person, and that he is incorporeal.[19] It might be
claimed that, if there is a Creator at all, he must be incorporeal,
on the ground that a physical body could not exist prior to the
existence of the universe of physical bodies; though it is not immediately apparent why the same should not apply to a mind or
disembodied person. What reason could there be for claiming
that such a being exists? Sometimes, in maintaining that God is a
necessary being, apologists plead that they are not getting themselves entangled in the fallacies of the ontological argument; what
they say they mean is that God 'is a being, and indeed the only
being, that contains in itself the reason for its own existence'. But
it is hard to see how such a definition could be instantiated. If one
means by a reason a logical ground, the point could only be that
that God exists follows from *what* God is, which is precisely the fallacy of the ontological argument. On the other hand, if what is
being alluded to is a cause rather than a logical reason, 'it is hard
to see what sense can be attached to the proposition that something causes itself. What is the difference, one may ask, between
saying that something causes itself and saying that it has no
cause?'[20]

The assumption which seems to underlie this kind of argument
is 'that the world cannot just happen to exist in the way it does'.
Now it is true that we are able to excogitate theories which account for observable facts; but the constituent propositions of
these theories are themselves contingent, themselves merely a
matter of fact; and if the theories are cast as deductive systems, it
can only be a contingent fact that the axioms of these systems are
true. The question why a scientific law obtains may be answered
by appeal to another scientific law; but however far we pursue the

question it inevitably arises again in the same form. A satisfying answer will 'be forthcoming only if the final explanation is found in the existence of a deity *whose actions proceed from his nature* and whose nature could not be different from what it is' (italics added). But such a search for an ultimate reason is not really coherent. Suppose we attribute purposes to God to account for how the world is organised. Either these are themselves as contingent, as much demanding explanation, as what was supposed to be explained by them; or one will have to say that God, in accordance with his nature, is bound to have such purposes. But thus attributing necessity to God's actions is to deprive them of any explanatory role. From necessary propositions, only necessary propositions follow; these are compatible with anything that might happen, and therefore cannot provide any explanation of what actually does happen. 'If it were rational to settle for an explanation of this sort, the reason would not be that it did away with contingency, but that it made sense of our experiences in a way that scientific theories did not. But then it would have to be shown that this was so.'[21]

Ayer's strictures on theistic arguments seem to me largely justified as far as they go; but do not touch arguments of the type that I have advanced. It is worth noting immediately that God, in accordance with that argument, will be part of what Ayer would call 'the secondary system', to be invoked in explanation of states of affairs which we can observe. Theism makes sense, if not of our 'experience' in the narrow sense, at least of the fact that our world is subject to investigation by scientific methods, in a manner that scientific theories themselves in the nature of the case cannot do. Ayer is perfectly correct that, however far one goes in the explanation of contingent facts, one never arrives at a 'necessary truth', in the sense of one that cannot be denied without self-contradiction. But, as conceived as conclusion of the kind of argument that I have advanced, God's existence is not a 'necessary truth' in this sense. It is *non-contingent, in the sense that* if there existed a being on whose understanding and will all else depended, its own existence could not be *contingent on* that of anything else.

It is claimed by Ayer that if one insists on regarding the course of world events as due to God's decision, one will be compelled to explain the decision as due to his essential nature.[22] But this seems to depend either on inadvertence to or on misapplication of the basic analogy, of the relation between the human agent and his actions and products, which appears to be at issue in argument from the world to God. God's decision to create the kind of world which he has created, or to create at all, is presumably *in accordance with* his nature in the sense that he does not *go against* his nature in thus deciding; but not in the sense that, given his nature, he *could not but have* thus decided. To conceive God's creativity in such a way is to apply a common-sense assumption about human agency; that people sometimes do things when they really could have done otherwise, even when all the circumstances are taken into account. I have already tried to show that philosophical arguments which purport to show that this assumption is erroneous are themselves based upon a mistake.[23]

I conclude that careful consideration of the arguments of Ayer's *The Central Questions of Philosophy* tend rather to strengthen than weaken the case for which I have argued in this book.

Notes and References

INTRODUCTION

1. *Immanuel Kant's Critique of Pure Reason*, tr. N. Kemp Smith, 500; A 590–1, B 618–9.

CHAPTER 1: ON THE ALLEGED UNIMPORTANCE OF ARGUMENTS FOR GOD'S EXISTENCE

1. Among the most interesting of many recent defenders of this view is D. Z. Phillips. Cf. *The Concept of Prayer* (London, 1965).

2. This standpoint is characteristic of Karl Barth. Cf. *Church Dogmatics* (Edinburgh, 1936–1964) 1, 2, 172f., 204, 232, etc.

3. This view has been popular among Protestant theologians since the publication of F. D. E. Schleiermacher's *On Religion* (New York, 1958) in 1799.

4. For a nice summary of the difficulties, see A. G. N. Flew, 'Death', in A. G. N. Flew and A. C. MacIntyre (eds), *New Essays in Philosophical Theology* (London, 1955) 267–72.

5. For this paragraph, cf. H. A. Hodges, *God Beyond Knowledge* (London, 1979).

6. Ibid., 171.

7. A. G. N. Flew, *The Presumption of Atheism* (London, 1976) 22.

8. C. Hartshorne, *A Natural Theology for Our Time* (New York, 1967) 32.

9. Cf. Bernard Lonergan, *Philosophy of God, and Theology* (London, 1973) 50–5.

10. Cf. Lonergan, *A Second Collection* (London, 1974) 28: 'What is decisive is not the felt presence, but the rational judgment that follows upon an investigation of the felt presence.'

11. Austin Farrer, 'The Christian Apologist', in Jocelyn Gibb (ed.), *Light on C. S. Lewis* (London, 1965) 26.

129

12. David Hay, 'More Rumours of Angels', *The Month,* vol. VII, no. 12 (December 1974) 803.

13. J. Macquarrie, *Principles of Christian Theology* (London, 1966) 45–52.

14. J. J. Shepherd, *Experience, Inference and God* (London, 1975) 2.

15. Don Cupitt, *Jesus and the Gospel of God* (Guildford and London, 1979) 92.

CHAPTER 2: STANDARD ARGUMENTS AND COUNTER ARGUMENTS

1. Cf. Paul Edwards, 'The Cosmological Argument', in D. R. Burrill (ed.), *The Cosmological Arguments* (New York, 1967) 106.

2. Cf. Bertrand Russell, *A History of Western Philosophy* (London, 1946) 610. Cf. also W. I. Matson, *The Existence of God* (Ithaca, 1965) 56–60.

3. Edwards, 'Cosmological Argument'.

4. *Summa Theologica,* I, ii, 3.

5. Edwards, 'Cosmological Argument', 104–5.

6. Ibid., 112.

7. There is a sense in which 'Process' theologians, such as A. N. Whitehead and C. Hartshorne, affirm the existence of other ultimate causes of things besides God. But an analogous argument would apply to them. By a 'sound' argument is meant here one which both is formally valid, and has premises all of which are true.

8. Edwards, 'Cosmological Argument', 106.

9. Cf. Hume, *An Enquiry Concerning Human Understanding* (London, 1902) Section VII.

10. Cf. L. Wittgenstein, *Tractatus Logico-Philosophicus* (London, 1961) 5.1361.

11. A. Schopenhauer, *The Fourfold Root of the Principle of Sufficient Reason*; cited Edwards, 'Cosmological Argument', 110.

12. T. Penelhum, 'Divine Necessity', in Burrill, *Cosmological Arguments,* 146.

13. Hume, *Dialogues Concerning Natural Religion,* IV.

14. D. R. Burrill, 'Introduction' to Burrill, *Cosmological Arguments,* 13.

15. Ibid., 14.

16. Kant, *Critique of Pure Reason* (CPR in subsequent notes) A 609, B 637; Kemp Smith's translation (KS in subsequent notes) 511.

17. Russell, *History of Western Philosophy*, 610–11.

18. A. Plantinga, 'Necessary Being', in Burrill, *Cosmological Arguments*, 137.

19. Ibid., 138.

20. Ibid., 141.

21. P. F. Strawson, *The Bounds of Sense* (London, 1966) 219.

22. Burrill, 'Introduction', *Cosmological Arguments*, 19.

23. Cf. P. T. Geach, 'Aquinas', in G. E. M. Anscombe and P. T. Geach, *Three Philosophers*, (Oxford, 1961) 112–13.

24. Hume, *Dialogues*, IX.

25. Burrill, 'Introduction', *Cosmological Arguments*, 16.

26. This was maintained by many nineteenth-century atheists, such as Büchner and Haeckel. Cf. Edwards, 121.

27. M. K. Munitz, *The Mystery of Existence*; cited J. Macquarrie, *Thinking About God* (London, 1975) 32.

28. Burrill, *Cosmological Arguments*, 18.

29. Penelhum, 'Divine Necessity', 154–5.

30. As William L. Rowe points out, the cosmological argument has two parts, the first of which attempts to establish the existence of an unchanged changer, a first cause, a 'necessary' being, or whatever; the second purporting to show that this is none other than God. Cf. *The Cosmological Argument* (Princeton and London, 1975) 5–6.

31. Edwards, 'Cosmological Argument', 103–4.

32. Strawson, *Bounds of Sense*, 229. Cf. Kant, CPR.

33. Strawson, ibid., 230.

34. Cf. Geach, 'Aquinas', 109.

35. Fr. Copleston remarks that Aquinas avoids sweeping generalisations; thus he does not say, in connection with the First Way, that *all* things in the world are moved or changed, or that *all* finite things come into being and pass away in connection with the Third. Cf. Copleston, *Aquinas* (Harmondsworth, 1955) 117.

36. That this is the point of the Fifth Way appears more clearly in the version in the *Summa Contra Gentiles* (I, 13) than in the *Summa Theologica*. Cf. Copleston, *Aquinas*, 112.

37. I have numbered the premises and steps for convenience of reference.

38. Plato, *Laws*, x, 891D–897B.
39. Ibid., 886D: 'It is . . . the novel views of our modern scientists that we must hold responsible for the mischief.'
40. I take it that the Athenian Stranger is Plato's mouthpiece.
41. Cf. R. G. Bury's translation (London and New York, 1952): 'The self-moving motion is the starting-point of all motions and the first to arise in things at rest and to exist in things in motion' (895B). ' "Self-movement" is the definition of that very same substance which has "soul" as the name we universally apply to it' (896A). 'Soul drives all things in heaven and earth and sea by its own motions' (896E).
42. Plato lists the 'motions' of 'soul' as 'wish, reflection, forethought, counsel, opinion true and false, joy, grief, confidence, fear, hate, love, and all the motions that are akin to these' (loc. cit.).
43. In the following questions, Aquinas goes on to argue that the 'prime mover' has the other characteristics typically ascribed to God by theists.
44. On his view, I used to be a boy in act and a man potentially, and am now a man in act and a corpse potentially.
45. 'Motion' in the natural modern sense is what Aquinas would describe as 'local motion'.
46. W. Kaufmann, *Critique of Religion and Philosophy* (New York, 1958) ch. v; cited Burrill, *Cosmological Arguments*, 3.
47. Cf. J. F. Ross, *Philosophical Theology* (Indianapolis and New York, 1969) 160.
48. A. Kenny, *The Five Ways* (London, 1969) 8.
49. Ross, *Philosophical Theology*, 162.
50. Spinoza, *Ethics* (London, 1910) part I, definition I.
51. Cf. A. Plantinga, *God and Other Minds* (Ithaca NY, 1967) 6–7.
52. Cf. J. J. C. Smart, 'The Existence of God', *New Essays in Philosophical Theology* (London, 1955) 38.
53. This interpretation is defended notably by Peter Geach ('Aquinas', 115) and Patterson Brown ('St Thomas' Doctrine of Necessary Being', *Philosophical Review* (1964) 82, 85). My own opinion, for what it is worth, is that this interpretation is the correct one. What Aquinas supposes from (vi) onwards, and in fact believed, that there were 'necessary' beings which derived their 'necessity' from some other being, seems to make little sense on

the other interpretation, but to be perfectly intelligible on this one.

54. Cf. p. 13 above.

55. Cf. Rendell N. Mabey, Jr, 'Confusion and the Cosmological Argument', *Mind* (1971) 124–6.

56. Kenny, *Five Ways*, 80.

57. Ibid.

58. Ibid., 81; cf. Ross, *Philosophical Theology*, 166.

59. Ross, *Philosophical Theology*, 167.

60. This is obviously not the place to go at length into physico-theological arguments; but is seemed suitable to deal briefly with the Fifth Way for the sake of completeness.

61. Cf. Ross, *Philosophical Theology*, 168.

62. Ibid., 169.

63. Kenny, *Five Ways*, 118.

64. Aquinas, In Physica, ii, 259.

65. Kenny, *Five Ways*, 118–19.

66. William H. Baumer, 'Kant on Cosmological Arguments', *The Monist* (1967) 528.

67. Ibid., 527.

68. Ibid., 528.

69. Anselm, *Proslogion*, 3.

CHAPTER 3: ON KNOWLEDGE AND EXPERIENCE

1. Plato, *Theaetetus*, 151E, 200E, 202C, 210A–B.

2. I prescind for the moment from the problem, which is at most marginal to my argument here, of whether what I directly apprehend in experience is a pattern of sensations, or a physical state of affairs. What *is* important in this context is that this experience does constitute what is in some sense a basis for much of what is generally taken to be knowledge.

3. It would not be admitted by those 'behaviourists' who would claim that thoughts and feelings are nothing over and above dispositions to observable behaviour. On reasons for not being a 'behaviourist' in this sense, see pp. 26–9 below.

4. For examples of the reasoning involved in this kind of case, see M. P. Crosland (ed.), *The Science of Matter* (Harmondsworth, 1971) 387–97.

5. Ibid., 392, 394–6.

6. A. J. Ayer seems at one time to have come close to this view; see *Language, Truth and Logic* (London, 1958) 101–2.

7. For this terminology, see B. J. F. Lonergan, *Method in Theology* (London, 1971) 20ff. A thorough account of the nature of these operations, and their bearing on philosophy and the sciences, is to be had in the same author's *Insight. A Study of Human Understanding* (London, 1957).

8. See *Insight*, 82–3, 248, 252, 269–70, etc. From this point of view, it may be suggested that the lack of attention to the role of questioning in the acquisition of knowledge has been a defect in much traditional and modern epistemology, in spite of the good start given in Plato's early *Dialogues* and in book II of Aristotle's *Posterior Analytics*.

9. For all the brilliance of the early Greek natural scientists, it would now be generally agreed that their beliefs on the subject were largely wrong. But no one doubts the truth of the reports about their immediate environments which Xenophon or Caesar seem to make in good faith.

10. Cf. Lonergan, *Method in Theology*, 16–17.

11. L. Wittgenstein, *Tractatus Logico-Philosophicus* (London, 1961) 1.

12. Ibid., 1.1.

13. Cf. Descartes, *Meditations on First Philosophy* (New York, 1960); especially the First and Sixth Meditations.

14. I.e., in some 'sense-datum' or 'sense-content', which certain philosophers would argue to be in some sense identical with some state of the brain.

15. Cf. P. L. Berger and T. Luckmann, *The Social Construction of Reality* (Harmondsworth, 1971) 13ff.

16. P. F. Strawson, *The Bounds of Sense* (London, 1966) 250.

17. For a useful discussion of the various meanings of 'induction', see R. Swinburne's 'Introduction' to *The Justification of Induction*, ed. Swinburne (London and Oxford, 1974).

18. David Hume, *A Treatise of Human Nature* (London and Glasgow, 1962) book I, part III, section XII; *An Enquiry Concerning Human Understanding* (London, 1902) section IV, part II.

19. Cf. A. J. Ayer, *The Concept of a Person* (London, 1963) 87–90, 104–11.

20. See Swinburne, 'Introduction', 1–2.

21. I do not think there is any contradiction of substance between the positive account of the role of induction in coming to know given here and Sir Karl Popper's well-known attack on induction (cf. K. R. Popper, *Objective Knowledge* (London, 1972) 85–103, 145–6, etc.; Bryan Magee, *Popper* (London and Glasgow, 1973) ch. 2). It may amount to much the same thing to say that types of reasoning often known as 'inductive' are to be justified in a way different to what is often supposed, and to attack 'induction'.

22. *The Collected Papers of C. S. Peirce*, ed. C. Hartshorne and P. Weiss (Cambridge, Mass., 1931–58) 5.189; quoted J. J. Shepherd, *Experience, Inference and God* (London, 1975) 146.

23. Hume, *Enquiry*, section IV, part I.

24. Memory is evidently notoriously fallible, unless one restricts the application of the concept in such a way that only those putative memories which are of actual past events which were witnessed by a person are really memories of his.

25. The principle of sufficient reason is more or less identical with the maxim of C. S. Peirce, that 'logic requires us to postulate of any given phenomenon, that it is capable of rational explanation' (*Collected Papers*, 5.265), and that 'it is never allowable to suppose the facts absolutely inexplicable' (cf. Shepherd, *Experience, Inference and God*, 147). I would prefer not to speak of 'logic' in this context, since the maxim does not seem to be a requirement of 'logic' in quite the usual sense of the term. There is nothing *self-contradictory* in the claim that some fact might be incapable of rational explanation, for all that, on my account, the contradictory of the claim is a corollary of principles which may be vindicated by demonstration of the fact that their contradictories are self-destructive.

26. Hume, *Enquiry*, section VIII. According to an understanding of causation very common among philosophers, 'C is a cause of E if and only if C and E are actual and C is *ceteris paribus* sufficient for E' (E. Sosa, *Causation and Conditionals* (Oxford, 1975) 1; Sosa cites J. S. Mill, R. B. Braithwaite, C. G. Hempel and K. Popper). Now that the existence or occurrence of C is *ceteris paribus sufficient for* the existence or occurrence of E may seem to entail that, if C exists or occurs, E *ceteris paribus cannot but* exist or occur. So at this rate it looks as though one must either accept universal determinism or deny the principle of sufficient

reason. However, I believe this to be a mistake. There is an equivocation which underlies the supposed dilemma, as has been pointed out by Professor G. E. M. Anscombe. The way of understanding 'sufficient condition' which I have just sketched is in fact not the only way. 'The phrase . . . cozens the understanding into not noticing an assumption. For "sufficient condition" sounds like, "enough". And one certainly *can* ask: "May there not be *enough* to have made something happen — and yet it not have happened?" ' (G. E. M. Anscombe, *Causality and Determination*; Sosa, *Causation and Conditionals*, 66). If I am right, the principle of sufficient reason does entail that, if any thing or state of affairs exists or occurs, there must have been *enough* to make it exist or occur; but not that it then *could not but have* existed or occurred. To use the jargon which I have introduced, it entails that everything must have enabling conditions, not that everything must be subject to causal necessitation. And in fact explanations of the former kind, as I bring out in the text, are accepted as adequate both in ordinary affairs and in science.

27. Descartes, *Meditations*; Second Meditation.

28. Cf. Lonergan, *Method in Theology*, 16–17. For an illustration of the same point, see N. Chomsky, 'A Review of Skinner's *Verbal Behaviour*', in *The Structure of Language*, ed. J. A. Fodor and J. J. Katz (New Jersey, 1964) 556.

29. The arguments of T. S. Kuhn's *The Structure of Scientific Revolutions* (Chicago, 1962) are often taken as tending to support this conclusion; cf. especially p. 169.

30. Cf. H. Meynell, 'On the Limits of the Sociology of Knowledge', *Social Studies of Science* (1977) 495–6.

31. See G. Grisez, *Beyond the New Theism* (Notre Dame, 1975) 44.

32. See K. T. Fann, *Wittgenstein's Conception of Philosophy* (Oxford, 1969) 54. I have to thank Philip Hoy for this reference.

33. Popper, *Objective Knowledge*, 17–20.

34. Ibid., 360.

35. Bryan Magee suggested this to me in conversation.

36. Magee, *Popper*, 47–8; Popper, *The Logic of Scientific Discovery* (London, 1972) 278.

37. See Kuhn, *Structure of Scientific Revolutions*, 169–70; P. K. Feyerabend, 'Consolations for the Specialist', in I. Lakatos and A. Musgrave (eds), *Criticism and the Growth of Knowledge* (Cambridge, 1970) 209.

38. Cf. H. Meynell, 'Feyerabend's Method', *Philosophical Quarterly* (1978) 245.

39. Kuhn goes so far as to say that 'if any and every failure to fit were ground for theory rejection, all theories ought to be rejected at all times' (*The Structure of Scientific Revolutions*, 145).

40. Thus I might say, for example in a psychology laboratory, 'I have a visual sensation as though of a tomato suspended about eighteen inches before my eyes'; rather than committing myself further, as I would in normal circumstances, by maintaining that there actually was such an object in this position.

41. Cf. A. J. Ayer, *Language, Truth and Logic* (London, 1958) 63–4, 123.

42. Cf. Bertrand Russell in *The Philosophy of Logical Atomism*: 'The things that we call real, like tables and chairs, are systems, series of classes of particulars, and the particulars are the real things, the particulars being sense-data when they happen to be given to you. A table or chair will be a series of classes of particulars, and therefore a logical fiction' (Bertrand Russell, *Logic and Knowledge*, ed. R. C. Marsh, 274).

43. Cf. Lonergan, *Insight*, 389, 391.

44. John Locke, *An Essay Concerning Human Understanding* (London, 1947) book II, ch. VIII. .

45. The qualification in brackets would leave room for those modern Lockeans who would acknowledge the tentative and provisional nature of actual scientific explanations. It is sometimes said that while science more or less demands that there be a distinction with regard to physical objects between their 'primary qualities' (what they actually have) and their 'secondary qualities' (what they merely seem to us to have due to the constitution of our sense-organs), philosophy is apt to show that such a distinction is untenable (cf. J. L. Mackie, *Problems from Locke* (Oxford, 1976) 7). It may easily be seen that the philosophical account presented here leads to no such conflict with science. By asking questions about things as presented to our senses, and known consequently in terms of their secondary qualities, we come to know of them as related to one another within an explanatory scheme, and as possessing qualities accordingly, which, while they do not directly correspond with what is available to our sense-experience, are verifiable by appeal to it. The more reliable such a scheme becomes in anticipating observations and successfully directing practice, the more it approximates

to describing things as they really are and would have been apart from human knowledge and sensation – in other words, to describing things in terms of their 'primary qualities'.

46. While the last sentence of the paragraph of course expresses Kant's view rather than Berkeley's, the rest of the paragraph represents more exactly the views of Berkeley. 'If . . . we consider the difference there is betwixt natural philosophers (i.e. scientists) and other men, with regard to their knowledge of the phenomena, we shall find it consists, not in an exacter knowledge of the efficient cause that produces them . . . , but only in a greater largeness of comprehension', and envisagement of 'general rules' which 'extend our prospect beyond what is present, and near to us, and enable us to make very probable conjectures, touching things that may have happened at very great distances of time and place, as well as to predict things to come' (G. Berkeley, *Principles of Human Knowledge*, cv; in *A New Theory of Vision and Other Writings*, ed. A. D. Lindsay (London, 1910) 165–6). W. V. O. Quine takes the point in effect, but jibs at its implications; cf. *From a Logical Point of View* (1963) p. 44: 'As an empiricist, I . . . think of the conceptual scheme of science as a tool, ultimately, for predicting future experience in the light of past experience. Physical objects are conceptually imported into the situation as convenient intermediaries—not by definition in terms of experience, but simply as irreducible posits comparable, epistemologically, with the gods of Homer. For my part I do, *qua* lay physicist, believe in physical objects and not in Homer's gods; and I consider it a scientific error to believe otherwise. But in point of epistemological footing the physical objects and the gods differ only in degree and not in kind. Both sorts of entities enter our conception only as cultural posits. The myth of physical objects is epistemologically superior to most in that it has proved more efficacious than other myths as a device for working a manageable structure into experience.' (I have to thank W. A. Mathews for drawing my attention to this passage.) Either Quine has good reason to prefer the conceptual scheme of science, as representative of the truth about things, to the Greek gods, or he has not. If he has, he is implicitly committed to what I have called the fully critical theory of knowledge. He has not, if he is consistent in his empiricism.

47. 'The Thing-in-itself . . . expresses the object, when we leave out of sight all that consciousness makes of it, all the deliv-

erances of feeling, and all specific thoughts about it. It is easy to see what is left, – utter abstraction, total emptiness, only describable still as a "beyond" – the negative of imagination, of feeling, and definite thought. Nor does it require much penetration to see that this *caput mortuum* is still only a product of thought, such as accrues when thought ends in abstraction unalloyed' (*The Logic of Hegel*, tr. W. Wallace (Oxford, 1874) 77).

48. Cf. Berger and Luckmann, *Social Construction of Reality*, 15.

49. Cf. David Bloor, *Knowledge and Social Imagery* (London, 1976) 36–8.

50. For a remarkable instance of the making of this point, together with a shrugging-off of the implications of so doing, cf. R. Bierstedt's 'Introduction' to Judith Willer, *The Social Determination of Knowledge* (Englewood Cliffs, New Jersey, 1971).

51. Cf. Meynell, 'On the Limits of the Sociology of Knowledge', 497.

52. M. K. Munitz, *The Mystery of Existence* (New York, 1965) 57–8, 61–2, 67–8.

53. Ibid., 68–70.

54. Ibid., 241–3, 247. For a concise presentation of the view of metaphysics just described, cf. F. Waismann, 'How I See Philosophy', *Contemporary British Philosophy*, 3rd series, ed. H. D. Lewis (London 1956) 489–90.

55. Cf. pp. 46–7 and Note 47 above.

56. Cf. pp. 31–2 above.

57. Cf. pp. 43–4 above.

58. Cf. pp. 44–8 above.

59. Munitz, *Mystery of Existence*, 58ff., 253.

60. Among such 'metaphysical' world-views I would include those whose proponents would prefer to label them as 'dialectical'. Cf. L. Bazhenov, 'Matter and Motion', in F. J. Adelmann (ed.), *Philosophical Investigations in the USSR* (Chestnut Hill and The Hague, 1975) 2–3.

61. In the sense in which physical objects can be said to be objects of sense-experience.

62. For a useful survey of conceptions of matter taken from the history of philosophy and science, cf. Crosland, *Science of Matter*; especially the 'Introduction', 23–32.

63. It seems to me that it is characteristic of Marxist philosophers to confuse this particular issue. But when this has been said, it ought to be added that the work of Soviet philosophers on

the concept of matter deserves more attention than it is usually given in the West; to judge at least from Bazhenov, 'Matter and Motion'.

64. See Berkeley, 'Three Dialogues Between Hylas and Philonous' (in Lindsay, *New Theory of Vision*, 203).

65. Hume, *Treatise*, book I, part III, sections II–IV, XIII, XIV; *Enquiry*, section VII. Aristotle, *Posterior Analytics*(Cambridge, Massachusetts and London, 1960) II, 1.

66. *Enquiry*, section II.

67. Ibid., section VII, part II.

68. Berkeley, 'Three Dialogues', 248–9.

69. *Enquiry*, section VII, part I.

70. Ibid., section XI, 115.

71. Hume, *Dialogues Concerning Natural Religion*, I–VIII (in *Hume Selections*, ed. Charles W. Hendel, Jr. (New York, 1955).

72. See especially section XII of the *Enquiry*, 116, concluding paragraph.

73. Cf. R. E. Hobart, 'Hume without Scepticism', *Mind* (July and October 1930).

74. Aristotle, *Metaphysics* (London, 1956) I,7; VII, 17.

75. In the *Posterior Analytics* (II, 1), Aristotle distinguishes four types of question; and then reduces these to two by pairing off the first and third, the second and fourth. Cf. B. J. F. Lonergan, *Verbum. Word and Idea in Aquinas* (London, 1968) 12–13.

76. See S. Körner, *Kant* (Harmondsworth, 1955) 28, 117–18.

77. For defences of scepticism in recent philosophical writing, see P. Unger, 'I Do Not Exist', *Perception and Identity*, ed. G. F. Macdonald (London, 1979); J. Kekes, 'The Case for Scepticism', *Philosophical Quarterly* (January 1975).

78. Aristotle, *Metaphysics*, IV, 4.

79. Wittgenstein maintained that knowledge of anything implied the possibility of doubt (*Philosophical Investigations* (Oxford, 1958) II, xi; 221–2).

80. P. 31–2 above.

81. For a recent and very skilful defence of the view that knowledge is without foundations, see M. Williams, *Groundless Belief* (Oxford, 1977).

82. P. 32 above.

83. For useful discussions of these issues, see G. J. Warnock (ed.), *The Philosophy of Perception* (London, 1967).

84. Perception of the stars would be a special case. If the star

as seen by the child or the savage is not where he supposes it to be, it is odd all the same to deny that he perceives the star.

85. See Williams, *Groundless Belief*, 22.

86. See Russell's paper, 'The Nature of Acquaintance', *Logic and Knowledge*, 127–74.

87. Wittgenstein, *Philosophical Investigations* (Oxford, 1958) ii, xi, 221–2.

88. See p. 63 above.

89. Wittgenstein, *loc. cit.*

90. David B. Burrell, *Aquinas. God and Action* (London, 1979) 4.

91. See R. Bambrough, 'How to Read Wittgenstein' in G. N. A. Vesey (ed.), *Understanding Wittgenstein*, (London, 1974) 130–1.

92. See p. 67 below. The conviction of the later Wittgenstein that 'it was language which linked thought to reality, not the other way round' (A. Kenny, 'The Ghost of the *Tractatus*', in Vesey, *Understanding Wittgenstein*, 11), does not seem to me to be an advance on his earlier view.

93. Kenny, 'Ghost of the *Tractatus*', 12.

94. Cf. Vesey, *Understanding Wittgenstein*, 'Foreword', xv; quoting P. Hacker.

95. J. Monod, *Chance and Necessity* (London, 1972) 154.

CHAPTER 4: EXPLANATION FOR INTELLIGIBILITY

1. Cf. A. G. N. Flew, *God and Philosophy* (London, 1966) 3.16: 'The other, when what is not the other is the universe, is hard to identify as anything but nothing.'

2. See above. A failure to make such distinctions seems to underlie the following remark by Stuart Hampshire: 'If you think of the fact of existence itself as a mystery, then you will soon find yourself looking for an explanation of the universe outside of the universe itself; in other words, you will look . . . for something beyond all existence which explains why anything at all exists' ('Metaphysical Systems', in *The Nature of Metaphysics*, ed. D. F. Pears (London, 1957); cited Munitz, *The Mystery of Existence*, 8–9).

3. The matter of this paragraph, and of several which follow, owes a great deal to conversations with H. V. Stopes-Roe.

4. N. L. Wilson, 'Existence Assumptions and Contingent Meaningfulness', *Mind* (1956) 343. See J. J. Shepherd, *Experience, Inference and God*, 26.

5. Shepherd neatly characterises the type of argument involved as 'transcendent-metaphysical abductive inference' (*Experience, Inference and God*, 150)..It is 'transcendent-metaphysical' by virtue of being what I have called second-order; it is 'abductive', in C. S. Peirce's terminology, as arguing from one fact to another supposed to supply an explanation for it.

6. See above.

7. T. R. Miles, 'On Excluding the Supernatural', *Religious Studies* (April 1966) 146–7; cited Shepherd, *Experience, Inference and God*, 8–9.

8. I have examined this question at greater length in *God and the World* (London, 1971) ch. 4.

9. Kai Nielsen, 'On Fixing the Reference Range of "God" ' *Religious Studies* (October 1966) 26–7; cited Shepherd, *Experience, Inference and God*, 19).

10. Cf. above.

11. Nielsen, 'On Fixing the Reference Range of "God" ', 27.

12. P. F. Strawson, *The Bounds of Sense*, 245.

13. Ibid., 236.

14. Ibid., 245.

15. For this reason, the move to explicitly materialist metaphysical positions by some recent analytic philosophers is to be welcomed. Cf. J. J. Smart, *Philosophy and Scientific Realism* (London, 1963); D. M. Armstrong, *A Materialist Theory of the Mind* (London, 1968); and A. Quinton, *The Nature of Things* (London, 1973).

16. Hume, *Dialogues Concerning Natural Religion*, viii (at the conclusion).

17. See pp. 60–1 above.

18. C. B. Martin, *Religious Belief* (Ithaca, 1959) 152–6; cited Shepherd, *Experience, Inference and God*, 42–3.

19. Cf. pp. 24–9, 42–5 above.

20. Kant, *Critique of Pure Reason*, 20; B xiii.

21. Ibid., 21; B xiv–xv.

22. Ibid., 21–2; B xv–xvi.

23. Ibid., 23; B xvii–xviii.

24. Ibid., 23; B xviii.

25. Ibid., 24; B xix–xx.

26. Ibid., 26; B xxiv–xxv.

27. Ibid., 28; B xxvii–xxviii.

28. Ibid., 29; B xxix–xxx.

29. See pp. 26–7, 31 above.

30. See pp. 42–4 above.

31. For a brief discussion of a possible solution, see Meynell, *God and the World*, 48–56.

32. Descartes, *Meditations*, Third Meditation.

33. Cf. pp. 31–2 above.

34. F. Nietzsche, *Thus Spake Zarathustra*, second part; 'On Self-Overcoming', in W. Kaufmann (ed.), *The Portable Nietzsche* (New York, 1954) 225. Kaufmann remarks, as well he may, that this passage raises many philosophical difficulties (193).

35. Pp. 25–7 above.

36. See J. Mepham, 'The Theory of Ideology in *Capital*', *Radical Philosophy* (1972) 12–13.

37. Ibid., 14.

38. See especially Armstrong, *Materialist Theory of the Mind*.

39. See Armstrong, *Belief, Truth and Knowledge* (Cambridge, 1973) *passim*.

40. This suggestion was made in conversation by Professor Dorothy Emmett.

41. T. Penelhum, 'Divine Necessity', in D. Burrill (ed.), *Cosmological Arguments*, 144–5.

42. Bertrand Russell said, 'You have to grasp this sorry scheme of things entire to do what you want, and that we can't do' (B. Russell and F. C. Copleston, 'The Existence of God. A Debate', in P. Edwards and A. Pap, *A Modern Introduction to Philosophy* (New York, 1973) 478.

43. Plato, *Meno*, 80 D–E.

44. On the mere pretence of doubting, see C. S. Peirce, in P. P. Wiener (ed.), *Values in a Universe of Chance* (Stanford, 1958) 40, 99.

45. See B. Lonergan, *Method in Theology*, 101–3; *Insight*, ch. XIX.

46. See Paul Edwards, 'The Cosmological Argument', in Burrill, *Cosmological Arguments* 117–18.

47. Ibid., 118.

48. Ibid., 120.

49. Penelhum, 'Divine Necessity', 145–6.
50. On this issue, as on so many others in the philosophy of religion, Flew is irresistibly quotable: 'In so far as causal explanation is interpreted ordinarily, the "vertical dimension" appears to be superfluous; while to the extent that some more exotic construction is provided, the quest for causes in this new sense cannot legitimately inherit the compulsiveness of the more workaday kind of inquiry' (Flew, *God and Philosophy*, 4.29).
51. Penelhum, 'Divine Necessity', 154.
52. See Strawson, *Bounds of Sense*, 212, 221; Kant, *Critique*, 308 (A 310, B 366) ff.
53. Strawson, *Bounds of Sense*, 221.
54. Ibid., 228.
55. Ibid.
56. Ibid., 231.
57. See pp. 26–7, 31–2 above.
58. See pp. 79–80 above.
59. See pp. 24–31 above.
60. For the claim that it can be fruitful, cf. Donald M. MacKay, *Science, Chance and Providence* (Oxford, 1978); W. H. Thorpe, *Purpose in a World of Chance* (Oxford, 1978). See also pp. 110–15 below.
61. See pp. 58–9 above.
62. See D. J. Allan, *The Philosophy of Aristotle* (London, 1952) 45–7.
63. The work of B. F. Skinner represents an heroic attempt to carry out this programme. Cf. his *Science and Human Behaviour* (New York, 1953).
64. Pp. 68ff. above.
65. Pp. 25–7 above.
66. Munitz, *Mystery of Existence*, 125.
67. *Kant's Inaugural Dissertation of 1770*, tr. W. J. Eckoff (New York, 1970) 69.
68. Ibid., 70.
69. Ibid., 71.
70. P. 86 above.
71. Strawson, *Bounds of Sense*, 221.
72. Kant, *Critique*, 490; A 575, B 603.
73. Strawson, *Bounds of Sense*, 222.
74. Ibid.
75. Kant, *Critique*, 495; A 583, B 611.

76. As opposed to change *vis-à-vis* its effects. Cf. Lonergan, *Insight*, 661–2.

77. As opposed, for example, to faith in what one believed on authoritative testimony.

78. A. C. Ewing, *Value and Reality* (London, 1973) 156–63.

79. Duns Scotus, *Reportata Parisiensia*, 1,2,2,6; cited J. F. Ross, *Philosophical Theology* (Indianapolis and New York, 1969) 174.

80. Ross, *Philosophical Theology*, 176.

81. For the notion of 'enabling conditions', see p. 38 above.

82. Anselm, 'Reply to Gaunilo' (*Anselm of Canterbury*, ed. and tr. J. Hopkins and H. W. Richardson, vol. i (London, 1974) 123–4). 'That than which a greater cannot be thought can only be thought to exist without a beginning. Now, whatever can be thought to exist but does not exist can be thought to begin to exist. Thus, it is not the case that that than which a greater cannot be thought can be thought to exist and yet does not exist. Therefore, if it can be thought to exist, it is necessary that it exist.'

83. See N. Rescher, *The Philosophy of Leibniz* (Englewood Cliffs, New Jersey, 1965) 66–7.

84. *Die Philosophischen Schriften von G. W. Leibniz*, ed. C. J. Gerhardt (Hildesheim, 1965) iv, 359, 406; cited Rescher, *Philosophy of Leibniz*, 67.

85. M. Schlick, 'Meaning and Verification', *Philosophical Review* (1936) 352; cited Munitz, *Mystery of Existence*, 8.

86. Munitz, *Mystery of Existence*, 33, 36, 41–2, 44.

87. See pp. 50–1 above.

88. Munitz, *Mystery of Existence*, 220, 222, 105.

89. See pp. 49–50 above.

90. Munitz, *Mystery of Existence*, 225–7, 232–4.

91. Ibid., 203, 206, 120, 152–3, 156–7.

92. Ibid., 212–13.

93. Ibid.

94. See pp. 71–76 above.

95. See pp. 73–4 above.

96. Munitz, *Mystery of Existence*, 220 ff.

97. Cf. pp. 36–9 above. The principle of sufficient reason would apply to all arguments supposed to establish states of affairs on the basis of evidence for them, and not merely to scientific arguments.

98. Munitz, *Mystery of Existence*, 206.

99. Cf. pp. 2–3 above.
100. Munitz, *Mystery of Existence*, 226–7.
101. Cf. pp. 31–3 above.
102. It does not *merely* involve a conceptual analysis, in my view, in that one has to advert to one's own cognitive procedures, and not simply analyse the correct use of the word 'know'.
103. See pp. 38–41 above:
104. Munitz, *Mystery of Existence*, 152–6.
105. See pp. 68–9 above.
106. Munitz, *Mystery of Existence*, 152–6.
107. Ibid., 156.
108. Ibid., 222.
109. Ibid., 157.
110. Ibid.
111. Ibid., 152.

CHAPTER 5: PARALIPOMENA

1. See p. 9 above.
2. See chapter 3 above.
3. See p. 36 above.
4. See pp. 93–7 above. It should be added that several beings of limited understanding do not explain what has to be explained; that is, a single field of causal relations intelligible in principle to an inquiring subject. If it were claimed that there might be several beings each of unrestricted understanding who shared the conceiving and willing, what would be the difference between such beings?
5. See p. 10 above.
6. See pp. 68–76 above.
7. Cf. A. Kenny, *The God of the Philosophers* (Oxford, 1979) 127: 'I know of no successful treatment of the philosophical problems involved in conceiving a non-embodied mind active throughout the universe.' Briefly, if there is any being that conceives and wills the universe as a whole, it cannot be a body, since nothing could be a body and not a *part* of the universe thus conceived and willed.
8. See pp. 53–4 above.
9. See p. 54 above.
10. See pp. 22–3 above.

11. See p. 18 above.

12. W. L. Craig, The *Kalām Cosmological Argument* (London, 1979).

13. Aristotle, *Physics*, III, 4–8. 202b30–208a20.

14. Aristotle, *Physics*, III, 6. 206a25–206b1.

15. Craig, *Kalām Cosmological Argument*, 10, 12, 27–8, 53, 55, 97, 103.

16. Ibid., 69, 70, 83, 86. For authorities in mathematical logic who support this view about the nature of the mathematical infinite, cf. 70.

17. Ibid., 44.

18. William L. Rowe says it is hard to see what is wrong with the argument, and turns to other matters (*The Cosmological Argument*, 122); John Hospers remarks that the difficulty of understanding how we got to the present moment, if an infinite number of moments had to elapse first, has not yet been resolved, and passes on to another topic (*Introduction to Philosophical Analysis* (London, 1967) 434). Cf. Craig, *Kalām Cosmological Argument*, 105.

19. Cf. pp. 73, 75 above.

20. On evidence supporting the 'big bang' theory of the origin of the universe, see Craig, *Kalām Cosmological Argument*, 111–16. See also S. Weinberg, *The First Three Minutes. A Modern View of the Origin of the Universe* (London, 1977). On the last point, cf. Craig, ibid, 122; citing J. Gribbin, 'Oscillating Universe Bounces Back', *Nature*, 259 (1976) 15.

21. Fred Hoyle, 'The Origin of the Universe'; cited Craig, *Kalam Cosmological Argument*, 118.

22. Hoyle, *Astronomy Today*; cited Craig, ibid.

23. Hoyle, *Astronomy and Cosmology*; cited Craig, ibid., 121.

24. See p. 72 above.

25. Thomas Aquinas was at pains to separate the question whether the world was created by God, from whether it had always existed. That it had not always existed, he thought, was to be held on faith alone. Cf. *Summa Theologica*, I, xlvi, 2.

26. R. Gruner, 'Science, Nature and Christianity' *The Journal of Theological Studies* (April 1975).

27. Ibid., 56ff.

28. Ibid., 59–60, 62.

29. Gruner, 'Science, Nature and Christianity', 60, 66, 68.

30. Ibid., 65.

31. For a convenient summary of the aspects of Aristotelianism objected to by Bacon, see R. Attfield, *God and the Secular* (Cardiff, 1978) 20–3.

32. *Posterior Analytics*, ii, 1–2, *Metaphysics*, vii, 17.

33. Francis Bacon, *Novum Organum*, i, 64; quoted Attfield, *God and the Secular*, 20.

34. From ii, 3 onwards of the *Posterior Analytics*, Aristotle is preoccupied with definition, demonstration and the use of syllogism.

35. For a survey of later 'Aristotelian' positions, see P. D. Kristeller, *Renaissance Thought* (New York, 1961) ch. 2.

36. P. 27 above. Aristotle's distinction between two fundamental types of question is preserved in the distinction, familiar to theorists of scientific method, between the concocting and testing of scientific hypotheses. 'In his endeavour to find a solution to his problem, the scientist may give free rein to his imagination, and the course of his creative thinking may be influenced even by scientifically questionable notions . . . Yet, scientific objectivity is safeguarded by the principle that while hypotheses and theories may be freely invented and *proposed* in science, they can be *accepted* into the body of scientific knowledge only if they pass critical scrutiny, which includes in particular the checking of suitable test implications by careful observation or experiment' (C. G. Hempel, *Philosophy of Natural Science* (Englewood Cliffs, New Jersey, 1966) 16).

37. Michael B. Foster, 'The Christian Doctrine of Creation and the Rise of Modern Natural Science', reprinted in C. A. Russell (ed.), *Science and Religious Belief* (London, 1973) 311ff.

38. Gruner, 'Science, Nature and Christianity', 67–8.

39. I.e., one with the qualifications outlined on pp. 88–9.

40. The difficulty may be resolved, in principle, if one regards the Bible as on the whole conveying in dramatic and pictorial terms the same truths as are more literally and technically expressed in the dogmas of the Church. For this view of the matter, cf. J. H. Newman, *An Essay on the Development of Christian Doctrine* (London, 1890) 190; and B. J. F. Lonergan, *Insight*, 739–40; and *Method in Theology*, 306–12, 319.

41. In reference to the work of the scientist, the late Dr J. Bronowski put it that 'order must be discovered, and in a deep sense it must be created' (*Science and Human Values* (London, 1961) 25).

The theoretical scientist must be fertile in *creating* orders which may possibly characterise the real state of affairs which gives rise to his data, and must stringently test his creations in relation to those data, if he is progressively to *discover* the real divinely-bestowed order which is already within things.

42. R. Taylor, *Metaphysics* (Englewood Cliffs, New Jersey, 1963) 87–9.

43. P. T. Geach and G. E. M. Anscombe, *Three Philosophers* (Oxford, 1961) 112–13.

44. See pp. 68–9 above.

APPENDIX

1. A. J. Ayer, *The Central Questions of Philosophy* (London, 1973).

2. Cf. Handel's *Judas Maccabaeus*, Act III: Through slaughter'd troops he cut his way/To the distinguish'd elephant.

3. See p. 27 above.

4. Ayer, *Central Questions*, 24–5, 31, 32.

5. Ibid., 34.

6. My italics.

7. Ibid., 89, 106–8.

8. Ibid., 84–5, 87–8, 110–11.

9. Ibid., 4.

10. Ibid., 12.

11. P. 122 above.

12. P. 120 above.

13. P. 122 above.

14. P. 47 above.

15. Ayer, *Central Questions*, 89.

16. P. 122 above.

17. Pp. 42–4 above.

18. Ayer, *Central Questions*, 87.

19. Ayer also mentions emotions such as love and indignation as usually attributed to God; and remarks shrewdly that if God has emotions, and these are appropriate to their objects, he must surely be subject to change (ibid., 212). The question of how, and in what sense, God may be said to have feelings and be subject to change is something of a crux in contemporary systematic theology, for example between the 'Process Theologians' and their opponents. This is not the place to go into the matter; I have tried to

deal with it briefly in 'The Theology of Hartshorne', *Journal of Theological Studies*, April 1973).

   20.　Ayer, *Central Questions*, 212–13, 215.

   21.　Ibid., 215–17.

   22.　P. 127 above.

   23.　P. 94 above.

Name Index

DATE DUE

DEMCO 38-297